THE PRAYER OF JESUS

The Prayer of Jesus

THOMAS CORBISHLEY, S.J.

MOWBRAYS
LONDON & OXFORD

ISBN 0 264 66068 4

First published 1976
by A. R. Mowbray & Co Ltd
The Alden Press, Osney Mead
Oxford OX2 OEG

Text set in 11/12 pt Baskerville
and printed in Great Britain
by Richard Clay (The Chaucer Press), Ltd,
Bungay Suffolk

Contents

It is a dangerous error, surely very widespread among Christians, to think that the heart can pray by itself. For then we confuse wishes, hopes, sighs, laments, rejoicings—all of which the heart can do by itself—with prayer. And we confuse earth and heaven, man and God. Prayer doesn't simply mean to pour out one's heart. It means rather to find the way to God and to speak with him, whether the heart is full or empty. No man can do that by himself. He needs Jesus Christ.

Dietrich Bonhoeffer

INTRODUCTION

THERE are not a few books on the prayers of Jesus, commentaries on the Lord's Prayer, on the other passages in the gospels where he speaks of prayer or himself prays. The purpose of this book is to attempt to get behind the utterances of Jesus to his own spirit of prayer; what we may call his prayer-life. Manifestly, anyone who takes it upon himself to treat such holy ground is bound to lay himself open to a charge of presumption, if not blasphemy. Alternatively, in the light of much modern New Testament criticism, he will be laughed at for wasting his time on an exercise which has been pronounced to be impossible. Many scholars hold that there is very little we can know about the 'Jesus of history'. All we know is the 'Christ of faith', the figure drawn for us by the evangelists, using sources now lost to us, or, at best, severely mangled in the course of transmission. A widespread attitude of mind may be summed up in Bultmann's words: 'What went on in Jesus' heart I neither know nor do I want to know.' Other scholars, without going all the way with Bultmann, have yet come more and more to hold that, whatever may be the historical substance behind our present gospels, the evangelists were not concerned to paint a portrait of

Jesus so much as to distil a message. Indeed the message itself owes more to subsequent theological and sociological developments than it does to the actual words and actions of the man to whom it is attributed.

It is not in the nature of this present undertaking to discuss in any detail the prevailing attitude of mind in this area of biblical criticism. But this much needs to be said. Of course it is true that what matters for us is the Christian message, the Christian truth, the Christian faith. Yet, unless we have some sort of assurance that this is substantially identical with 'what went on in Jesus' heart', the importance of the life and work of Jesus is, to say the least, enormously diminished. We are of course committed to the view that the Risen Christ, a cosmic figure, reconciling the world, restoring all things, is immensely more significant than anything explicitly stated in the words of the itinerant preacher, living under the Emperor Tiberius and the governor Pilate. But equally we hold that all this universal truth developed out of, and is rooted in, the life and work of JESUS. His death occurred at a certain moment in time on a small hill outside Jerusalem. Its effects transcend time and space. Yet we need to nourish both our piety and our faith by going back to the temporal event and trying to understand it in its historical setting.

So is it with the actual teaching of Jesus. We are committed to the belief that Jesus is the supremely important vehicle of God's revelation. In him, in his life and teaching, we claim to have been given the final expression of the truth of God, in so far as that truth is accessible to the human mind. Our appreciation of the meaning of that truth is, of course, a developing thing. Certainly the contribution of the first generation of Christians, of the apostles and their heirs, the evangelists, was of special importance in that development. But unless the gospels as we have them, based on earlier documents or on other sources, are traceably connected with the actual teaching of Jesus, we have no assurance that they are in any real sense authentic, that they have not been in any way falsified, however much they may have been elaborated, in the later 'kerygma'—the Good News preached by the apostles and their heirs.

To what extent Jesus himself, at the level of his purely human awareness, appreciated fully the meaning of the pronouncements on which his followers built, may be arguable. But it is difficult to accept the view that the titles which were later attributed to him—Messiah, Son of God, Son of Man and the like—did not somehow reflect attitudes of his own mind. This is not to argue that the whole modern approach to New Testament studies is misconceived. It is simply a reminder that an involvement in the minutiae of form-criticism and the like may obscure more important and not less valid considerations. In the words of R. H. Fuller: 'It was because he was who he was that Jesus did what he did.'

In the context of our present concern, it was the whole spiritual experience of Jesus which was the dynamic of his later activity. And there is a further consideration to be borne in mind. We believe that, through the activity of the Spirit of God within us, we are in touch with Jesus Christ 'the same today as he was yesterday and as he will be for ever'. (Heb. 13.8) We are here beyond the range of scholarship or even theology. True, our scholarship and our theology must not be at variance with our personal religion, if this is not to be a vague and subjective affair of sentimental piety. Moreover, it is important not to mistake secondary considerations for primary ones. Equally, pure scholarship does not necessarily present the best approach to Christian practice. There are those who would discredit any attempt to picture to oneself what Jesus looked like on the grounds that, for example, we do not know whether his eyes were blue or brown. True enough; but we do know that he had two eyes, and that, in fact, they were more likely to be brown than blue, just as his skin was brown rather than white or yellow or black. We do not know with certainty the dates of his birth or his death. But we do know that these events did take place at a precise date; a date which can be established with some degree of probability. To say airily that we do not have the materials for a 'life of Christ' is to be a little too cavalier.

We know, for example, when he was born, to within a year or two. We know quite a lot about the religious world into which he was born. We know enough about the social and political situation of his world. We are therefore in a position to fill out the almost empty canvas of the years of the boyhood and early manhood of Jesus with a sufficient wealth of detail to enable the final portrait to be more complete and more convincing than the critics are prepared to admit. The mere external happenings of any life are of course significant only in so far as they illuminate the personality who is the subject of a biography. In the case of Jesus, concentration on the detailed events may obscure rather than illuminate what he was and what he stood for. To that extent we need not worry too much about the scarcity of factual information about the 'hidden years'. On the other hand, it is not in human nature to be content with a purely abstract and cerebral portrayal of the truths by which we live. The very fact of the Incarnation is God's recognition of a human need to see and to feel no less than to think and to argue. Faith in Jesus is ultimately faith in what he was rather than in what he said or did. Yet, just as our human love feeds on physical contact and verbal communication until it becomes independent of these channels—if it ever does—so is it with the love and the faith which are at the heart of our prayer-life. We are not, in fact, satisfied with the speculations of the most intelligent commentator on the Bible. They may help us to a better appreciation of the sacred text. They can never be a substitute for it.

So we can return with some assurance to our consideration of the spiritual development of Jesus. We do not propose to do this on the basis of gospel evidence, except in so far as this may be invoked to illustrate some suggestion. Nor do we claim that our approach is anything more than tentative. It is impossible for anyone to be sure about what is going on in the depths of another's personality. In the case of Jesus, the normal problems that arise when we seek to enter into the mind and heart of another human being are immensely increased by the fact that in him there existed an utterly unparalleled relationship with the Godhead. Nevertheless, it seems desirable that we should attempt this sort of study, if only because some appreciation of what prayer may have meant to him will not only enable us to come a little closer to some fellow-feeling with him but will also help to enrich our own prayer-life.

For this latter reason, it has seemed worth while to begin with a discussion of the experience of prayer as a common human activity. For, incomparably sublime as the prayer of Jesus was in comparison with the stumbling efforts of ordinary mortals, it must yet be seen to belong to the same broad type of human experience. Having looked at prayer, then, in the normal human situation, we shall turn to speculate on the way in which what we may call the prayer-life of Jesus may be thought to have developed. After that we shall be in a better position to appreciate the many passages in the gospels where his prayers are quoted.

I

THE EXPERIENCE OF PRAYER

BOOKS about prayer abound. They give us advice about how to pray, they list methods of prayer, they analyse for us our progress, they chart our future course, they draw up subjects for meditation. And here is an addition to their number; a book moreover which even presumes to talk about the prayer of Jesus himself. Manifestly, anything which can be said on that subject, whatever depth it may have, must yet fall infinitely below the reality it purports to expound. Nevertheless, such an undertaking need not be entirely valueless. After all, Jesus is, and must always be, for the Christian the great teacher of prayer. And if our prayer is to be more than a mere repetition of a set of formulas (not excluding the Lord's own Prayer), we can surely be helped by trying to enter, however inadequately, into the mind and heart of the Master himself as he prays.

Books about prayer abound. And they abound precisely because they deal with a subject which is of fundamental importance in the life of any Christian, indeed of any human being; for the exercise we call prayer is an expression of the deepest truth about any man (whether he consciously accepts it or not); his relationship with the Creator on whom he finally depends for his existence and for all that makes existence fruitful. If the analogy be not thought too frivolous, we may say that books about prayer abound in the way in which cookery books abound. The process of preparing food is basically simple. It consists in applying heat, in various forms, to the substances needed to supply the appropriate chemicals to the human body. But there is, as we know, a much more complex process involved in producing food that is both nourishing and appetising. It is a complex process because the human body itself is a complex organism, to say nothing of the fact that, for all their essential similarity, human beings vary so much amongst themselves that, proverbially, one man's meat is another man's poison.

But if the human body is astonishingly complex, what are we to say of the human psyche? The normal human face is made up of the same characteristic features—lips, eyes, nose and the rest—arranged in the same pattern. Yet how immensely different do human beings look. In the same way, we can catalogue the primary constituents of the human psyche—mind, memory, affections and so on—but the psychological differences between the individual members of the human race is immeasurably more bewildering than any merely physical dissimilarity.

If, then, pursuing our analogy, we regard prayer as the nourishment of the soul, it will follow that a variety of approaches will be called for. The essential ingredients are unchanging. The combination, the seasoning, the presentation, in a word the whole treatment, will necessarily and rightly vary. Some aspects of that treatment will appeal to one; they may be distasteful to another. Whilst it is to be hoped, for example, that everybody will find something helpful somewhere in this book, it is unlikely that everything in it will satisfy everybody. Nobody eats his way steadily through all the recipes in a cookery book.

The first point to be made, then, is that whilst all Christians, and indeed all men, are called to exercise prayer in some form, the actual way in which any given person prays is, or should be, individual and unique to that person. After all, prayer is, as we have already thought, an expression of a relationship between the individual and his God. Whilst God is the common Father of all mankind, the relationship between the unique individual that I am and the Being to whom I am related in a unique way is something that has no counterpart in the whole of creation.

Even at the level of everyday experience, how incommunicable is a man's reaction to a given stimulus. Two people may look at the same landscape from all but identical viewpoints. In one sense they are sharing the same experience, especially if they are close in mind as well as in body. Yet my seeing of that scene is mine, not his; his seeing is his, not mine. The relationship which links the landscape to my interpretative vision is wholly other than the relationship linking that same scene to my friend's vision. Nor is the difference in response due exclusively or even primarily to the fact that my friend and I differ in physiological equipment—his sight may be keener than mine; or personal interest—he may be a geologist and I a farmer;

or poetic sensitivity and so on. The ultimate basis of the difference is simply that I am I, and he is he. My seeing of what we both see is uniquely, incommunicably, mine.

So is it with the relationship that exists between myself and God. In the words of Teilhard de Chardin:

> By means of all created things, without exception, the divine assails us, penetrates and moulds us. We imagined it as distant and inaccessible, whereas in fact we live steeped in its burning layers.... As vast as the world and much more formidable than the most immense energies of the universe, it nevertheless possesses in a supreme degree that precise concentrated particularity which makes up so much of the warm charm of human persons.... God reveals himself everywhere only because he is the ultimate point upon which all realities converge. (*Milieu Divin*, pp. 112–14)

It may, of course, be objected that in the prayer of prayers, Our Lord encourages us to say *Our* Father. Does not this mean that we are all united with God in the same way, that our filial relationship is one that we all share? Of course; just as the children of one family are united in a filial relationship with their parents. Yet my love for my father is clearly not the same as the love my brother or sister feels for him. We are united in a common love, and distinguished by the individual loving that each of us experiences.

All this may seem to be labouring the obvious. Yet it is important and necessary to say it, precisely because we have all, to a greater or less extent, been encouraged to think that we can make a success of our prayer by modelling it on somebody else's way of praying. We read, hopefully, 'manuals' of prayer. We try to follow, admittedly from afar, the Way of Perfection; we explore, timidly, the Interior Castle; we study the Graces of Interior Prayer—and wonder how far we have got. And all the time, the danger is that this sort of investigation is distracting me from really praying, from putting myself in the presence of *my* God, in *my* way, with *my* needs, *my* aspirations, above all *my* love.

In an interesting lecture on 'Poetry and Dialectic' published in *The Night Battle* (pp. 119–49, esp. pp. 142–6) Professor J. M. Cameron asks the question: 'How do I learn to identify one of my sensations as a pain?' He goes on:

> The force of this question is brought out if we note that it is a prior condition of my applying the concept of pain to my own case that I should already know the meaning of the word 'pain'. But to say that the word 'pain' has a meaning is to imply that it is a unit in the public language and that my uses of the word and the uses of the word by others have the same range.

Now, true as this is at one level, it seems to leave out of account the fact that I can use words like 'pain', 'love', grief', 'ecstasy', meaningfully not simply because they are units in a 'public language', but because the private experience of them adds to our appreciation of them a quality that no amount of talk can give. In fact, Cameron admits as much when he says:

Because each of us is himself and not another, unique in his history and in his relations to others, a characterization of our individual feelings drawn from the common stock leaves us with a sense of injustice; for the feelings are rendered not in their particularity but in respect of their likeness to the feelings of others.

For our present purposes, the point to be made is that, too often people's prayer life is unsatisfactory precisely because they feel—perhaps out of a not unreasonable modesty—that they must copy other people's way of praying, using 'methods' they find in books, repeating set formulas; in a word not letting themselves be themselves. Yet, if ever a man or woman ought to be absolutely and uninhibitedly personal it is surely in the expression of a relationship which, as we have thought, is unique and unrepeated in the whole of the universe. 'Prayer' may be a 'unit in a public language', but our thoughts and feelings must be 'rendered in their particularity' if they are to be authentic.

In other words, the whole significance of praying is that it expresses *my* way of relating to *my* God. (We are not here concerned, of course, with communal worship, though of this two things should be said. The first is that the meaningfulness of communal worship will be enormously enhanced if the members of the worshipping community, in their togetherness, are already fully alive to the deep roots of true prayer. Secondly, as we shall see, one important feature of genuine prayer is that it does enable the one who prays to enter more fully into understanding relationships with others. It is because I am growing in what we can only call a 'sense of God' that I am driven to reach out to others whose being is not less truly grounded in the reality of which I am more and more conscious.)

For the vast majority, perhaps for everybody, prayer begins at the level of the spoken word. In our communications with our fellow human beings, words, written or spoken, are probably the commonest medium, even though sight and touch are often the most meaningful, especially at a certain level of intimacy. Unfortunately, God is invisible and physically unapproachable, so that we have to fall back on the only remaining means of presenting ourselves to him. Now the words we use, even if they are traditional forms, will become genuine prayers only if they express something of ourselves. In everyday life, as we know only too well, there are certain tired clichés which are the common coin of daily interchange. Yet the same words can take on a vivid meaningfulness when spoken with the conviction born of love. A guest leaving a party can say 'that was absolutely lovely', meaning no more than a polite and casual 'thank you'. The very same words, spoken in the context of a totally loving relationship, take on a quality of life that transforms them. In the same sort of way, even if we feel we cannot improve on the prayer formulas that others have devised, it will at least be desirable that we should try to look at them with our own eyes, in our own situation, to make sure that we really mean what they say. And the sooner I come to praying 'in my own words', the better is my vocal prayer likely to be.

For many people, too, prayer means what is

called 'intercessory prayer', asking God for something. It is becoming increasingly common for people to say or to think that this is really a rather meaningless exercise, since what is going to happen is already predetermined and that nothing I can do or say is going to change it. The weather, for example, is determined not by some arbitrary whim on God's part but by the prevailing meteorological situation. If a deep depression is approaching from the Atlantic, can I hope that, in response to my prayers, God will make it fill up and move away? Am I, in effect, praying for a miracle?

In tackling this question, it is important to begin by pointing out that such intercessory prayer is frequently recommended in the gospels, even whilst Jesus is also recorded as having said that God knows what we need, before we ask him (Matt. 6.8). Yet these very words are immediately followed by the Lord's prayer in which we are encouraged to ask for our daily bread. We shall have more to say about this prayer in a later chapter but in our immediate context it seems appropriate to point out that, here as elsewhere, Jesus seems chiefly concerned that we should be developing a sense of filial trust in our heavenly father. But that trust must be an absolute thing, not something dependent on whether or not he gives me exactly what I want here and now. If an earthly father is unlikely to give us a stone when we ask for bread, *a fortiori* our heavenly father will not let us down. If he does not give me just what I would like to have in this situation—a fine day for my wedding, the cure of a dear friend, even the success of a 'good cause'—can I go on believing that God's love is in no way less real, less genuine, than that of a human benefactor? Is my happiness something that depends less on the satisfaction of my immediate desires than on a growth in a capacity to see the larger context into which the immediate achievement of success or the getting what I feel I need at the moment may not necessarily fit?

In other words, it is perfectly reasonable that we should ask for things, simply because this is a natural expression of a filial attitude. But, if our love of God is a mere 'cupboard-love', it is a love that is unworthy of adult human beings. The conclusion of the debate in the book of Job, in which the latter was arguing with God because of what he regarded as unfair treatment, is highly relevant. I am the man who obscured your designs with my empty-headed words; I have been holding forth on matters I cannot understand or marvels beyond me and my knowledge (Job 42.3).

My asking for something is an expression of my trust in God. Whether or not I get this particular thing, I remain humbly confident of God's wisdom and God's love. In the meantime let us remember that our petitionary prayer, like all vocal prayer, is a primitive level of the total experience we are discussing.

Now, in the words of that great expert, Don John Chapman:

It is common enough for those who have any touch of 'Mysticism' (which I regard as having a natural base, though it is a grace if faithfully used) to be absolutely unable to find any meaning in vocal prayers. If you simply read them without praying, you can understand them as well as any other book. But if you turn to God, all thinking and understanding stops. I suppose this is because something else is going on.

What is going on is that we are being led on to realise that the words themselves and the relatively superficial meaning they bear can inhibit our appreciation of the deeper truth that lies 'behind'.

For words, any words, are significant only because they express ideas. Perhaps this is why our Lord tells us 'not to babble as the pagans do, for they think that by using many words they will make themselves heard' (Matt. 6.7). When the fourth gospel speaks about the Word, the author is not referring either to a sound or to a set of written signs. He is telling us of the Eternal Idea in the mind of God, the Idea which expresses the full truth about himself, and includes, mysteriously, the very pattern of that creation which 'came to be through him'. The more, then, we can dispense with language and learn to concentrate on what the words are trying to say, the more authentic will our prayer be.

Already, then, we are embarking on what is technically known as 'meditation'—the intellectual and imaginative approach, as against the purely verbal. (The term 'imaginative' refers to such practices as picturing the scene in which, for example, some gospel incident—the subject-matter of the meditation—is set.) It is, of course, true that words are inevitably accompanied by some measure of intellectuality if they are to be at all meaningful; equally, even the 'purest' idea will have attached to it some term, however shadowy. But the emphasis

24

is on the idea rather than on the corresponding ver-
balisation.

Many people seem to remain satisfied with 'meditation' for years, if not for a whole lifetime. Yet it
is probably true that clinging for too long to this
form of prayer may be due to a fear of giving it up,
a fear that can spring from a genuine humility, but
may also be the result of a reluctance to move from
familiar territory into the unknown and uncharted.
But the importance of making our prayer-experience as individual and personal as possible would
seem to require that we should be prepared to take
the next step. For that next step is the development
of a process which brings us face to face, not with
someone else's idea of God, but with God himself—
my God.

Again, a parallel with human relationships may
be helpful. When a young man falls in love with
a young woman, he is impelled, like Orlando:

to carve on every tree
the fair, the chaste, and unexpressive she.

He writes letters every day, perhaps several times
a day. If he cannot write poems himself, he copies
out a Shakespearean sonnet or a piece by John
Donne. He measures the intensity of his love by
the length of his verbal output. But, after marriage,
as the years pass, he finds that that sort of protesta-
tion is self-conscious and inadequate. A look, a
caress, can say much more than the most passionate
lyric. The turbulence of those early years has been
replaced by a state of mind which is one of more
profound and more enduring love, even though

perhaps it cannot be put into words. So often, as Pascal says, 'in love silence is worth more than speech'. There can, of course, be a silence of contempt, of embarrassment, of hostility. But the silence in which love expresses itself is all the more eloquent because it possesses a literally ineffable quality. When Browning spoke of 'fancies that broke through language and escaped', he was giving expression to a truth which we all recognise yet often fail to implement, the truth that the most profound realities are beyond our ability to put them into words.

Now if this is true at the level of our ordinary experience, how much truer must it be of our deeper concern with what Thomas Merton, in the spirit of an age-old tradition, calls 'the Real within the real'. The basic facts on which the whole universe is structured are indefinable and indescribable. They are thus indefinable because definition is always in terms of something simpler, more ultimate. There are certain terms that we all use intelligently, though we should be baffled if we were asked to define what we meant by, say, 'here and now', 'giving and receiving', 'thinking' and a score of other expressions.

One of the most fundamental of all our ideas is that of being or existing. Manifestly, it is impossible to *explain* this idea to anyone who asks for an explanation. All we can do is to point to the fact that the questioner already exists and must know that he exists even before asking the question. But, if it is impossible to describe or define what the term means, this by no means implies that we cannot grow in an awareness of it. And we grow in such an awareness by a kind of wordless contemplation of different versions of it. For myself, 'I am' is the fundamental truth. Yet, if I truly love, 'you are' is seen to be at least as important a fact. But this fact becomes more meaningful to me not by philosophical speculation about its logical status but by a determined effort to contemplate it, to look at it or, rather, at the 'you' in question. Mutual awareness is the radical experience that is the very foundation of a loving relationship. Beyond philosophy, beyond any kind of imagining or conceptualisation, in a wordless attitude of sheer attention, however much it may be mediated through word or touch or look, human love is achieved by a total self-giving in which each discovers the other and yet finds himself; herself.

Such would seem to be the human analogue of the deeper experience of genuine prayer. For in such prayer my naked self, that 'me' which, for all its similarities to a million other human beings, is yet unique in its unlikeness to any other creature from the beginning to the end of history, encounters the indescribable, unimaginable, incomprehensible yet absolutely real person we call God. This God is not just a loving being; he is the sheer power of love itself. Now when we say 'love' we need to recall that we are not talking of some emotional reaction such as, with us, often passes for love. The emotional attitude may indeed accompany and help to promote true love. Of itself it is, as we know, evanescent. Genuine love is an abiding attitude of unselfregarding, outgoing generosity. When, therefore, we speak of God as love, we mean that the ultimate truth about reality in that at its heart is one whose whole nature is to give, to enrich, to create. For the only possible answer to the question: Why does anything exist at all? is simply that essential Being is essentially creative.

In the encounter of prayer I discover this truth, not as an intellectual proposition but as an experienced activity. I come to see that what ultimately makes sense is this fact of an ever-springing fountain of inexhaustible unselfishness. I see myself as constituted by the activity of this flowing generosity. I also recognise that, whilst I have not, could not, make any contribution myself to my own coming-to-be, I have, nevertheless, been made capable of adding my own contribution to the ongoing task of propagating still wider the life-giving power of divine love. In my relationship to God I am the sheer recipient; the object of his love. What is true of myself I recognise to be true of all my fellow-men. We are all equally poor of ourselves, equally rich through the divine bounty. I recognise, too, that it is possible for me either to impede or to hasten the flow of God's blessings.

All this becomes clear to me, not as the result of any reasoning process, but by allowing myself to be totally open to the divine influence. After all, I do not argue myself into loving another human being. I love that other because of what she is. I can come to know her, it is true, only through the medium of her words, her smile, her eyes. I may come to love her because of her beauty. But:

Love's not time's fool, though rosy lips and cheeks
Within his bending sickle's compass come;
Love alters not with his brief hours and weeks. . . .

The deep reality of an abiding human love has about it something that is independent of the passing years. It is a witness to a reality beyond itself. Bernard Shaw makes one of his characters say:

> When you loved me I gave you the whole sun and stars to play with. I gave you eternity in a single moment, strength of the mountains in one clasp of your arms, and the volume of all the seas in one impulse of your soul.

Even that cynic would recognise the power of love between mortals.

It is scarcely surprising that the encounter of the human soul with the very spirit of love should have effects beyond our wildest imaginings. Yet we are surprised. We are surprised because we lack faith in the tremendous reality of the sheerly spiritual. Earth-bound and material-minded, we are reluctant to surrender to the appeal of anything we cannot touch or see. Yet, if our professions of faith are more than mere parrot-repetitions of hackneyed phrases, we must recognise that we are committed to accepting the existence of a whole dimension of reality beyond our human sight. We murmur 'God is love'. We may even hear sermons preached on the subject. But, whilst we appreciate the power of love in human affairs, we seem incapable of raising our sights to contemplate the mere possibility of such a power increased to infinity.

Only in and by the experience of prayer can we become convinced of all this. For in prayer we seek to lose sight of ourselves in an awareness of the Other who is God. In the words of Thomas Merton:

The consciousness of Being ... is an immediate experience that goes beyond reflexive awareness. It is not 'consciousness of' but *pure consciousness* in which the subject as such disappears.

Elsewhere he says:

the empirical self [by which he means the self as we experience it in ordinary life] is seen by comparison to be 'nothing', that is to say contingent, evanescent, relatively unreal, real only in relation to its source and end in God, considered not as object but as free ontological source of one's own existence and subjectivity.

Perhaps this sort of language suggests that we are here dealing with a very 'advanced' form of prayer. The truth is that we begin to pray in any real sense of the word only when we have gone beyond a dependence on formulas or even concepts and ideas. There is, it is true, a sense in which we can never totally dispense with words and ideas. But these are like the scaffolding we need in order to put a building. What matters is the building, not the scaffolding. In this life, since the building will never be complete, the scaffolding will always be needed. But it must always be seen as subordinate to the building itself.

To put it another way, progress in prayer means a progressive simplification of our 'way' of praying. From words and formulas to ideas and concepts we continue, as it were, to 'get behind' words or ideas to their underlying meaning. For, after all, words and concepts are, as Cameron says, units in a 'public language'. But, in the essentially private relationship which prayer expresses, we want to get away from anything that might seem to intrude. Chesterton, in an exaggeration which yet indicates a profound truth, says: 'No man who is in love thinks that anybody has been in love before. No woman who has a child thinks there have been such things as children.' The exaggeration is clear. Yet the underlying truth consists in the fact that *this* love of mine, *this* child of mine, is so utterly unique that it is as though there were nothing like it in the whole of creation. There *is* nothing quite like it.

In the same way, what my prayer means is that I am coming to appreciate the wonder of my relationship with the One who is both utterly unique in himself and with whom I am linked in a bond that is unrepeated and unrepeatable. The poet, Gerard Manley Hopkins, coined the term 'inscape' to express the 'selfhood', the pattern or design of this particular leaf, cloud, stone, which constitutes it this and no other thing. It is the inner reality which finds outward manifestation in a number of qualities which, in one sense, it shares with all the other members of the species to which it belongs. Yet, because the inner reality is what this particular thing is, even the outward manifestation is unrepeatable. The pattern of two leaves may be very similar; they are never identical. One critic defines 'inscape' as the 'core of creative purposiveness' which underlies the pattern and gives it the unity which it possessses.

Now if this is true of inanimate nature or of living things at the sub-human level, it is immensely truer of human beings. Each of us may be capable of appreciating his own inscape. Through the experience of love I come to some awareness of the inscape of my beloved. But, in the end, I am known in my uniqueness to God and God alone. Deeper than any sensation, more abstract than any thought, prior to any conscious act of will, I lie open to the loving creative act of God, without which I am literally nothing, by means of which I come into existence. I am. And I recall that this is also the primordial utterance of God himself. Here we are at the very heart of our relationship. God is totally Other since, unlike me, he is, absolutely, by no-body's favour. He is simply because that is what he must be. I am simply by his favour. And yet, I am. I am because, and only because, he already is.

It is through prayer, what is sometimes called the prayer of simple regard, that I come to an effective appreciation of this two-sided truth. I become aware of the abiding reality, the reality as presented to me in and through my day-to-day experience. That is why, at least periodically, it is necessary for me to withdraw from the routine of daily life, with its imperious demands on my attention. Obviously, such a withdrawal will often have to be brief and temporary. Yet I will never come to pray in the fullest sense of that word unless I have opportunities, however brief, to retire into a place apart, undisturbed by the telephone, the social call, the television screen. A French active social worker has said 'a journey of four stations on the Metro is our desert'. It is not, as we shall see, that these things do not have their proper place in life. But we shall be in a better position to see what that proper place is, the more we are able to relate them to the abiding realities, the eternal verities.

Traditionally, as we begin to pray, we 'put our-selves in the presence of God'. What does this mean? After all, there is an important sense in which we are never out of God's presence. In the words of the Psalmist:

If I take the wings of the morning and remain in
  the uttermost parts of the sea,
Even there also shall thy hand lead me: and thy
  right hand shall hold me.
If I say, Peradventure the darkness shall cover
  me: then shall my night be turned to day ...
The darkness and light to thee are both alike.
  (Ps. 139)

What such passages mean, of course, is that we are always present to the mind of God. What we have to do when we enter upon our prayer is to make God consciously present to ourselves. How this is to be done will, as always, depend on the temperament, the experience, the training of the individual. For some it will mean picturing some scene with re-ligious associations. There are those who find a musical phrase helpful and evocative. Others again will make use of a familiar text, a fragment of a psalm, of St Paul or St John. For those who have had long training in prayer-discipline it will be largely a matter of shutting out sights or sounds or even ideas, approaching the silent emptiness that is yet the fulness of God's reality. Indeed for some this will be their prayer.

But for the others, what comes next? Clearly, the only possible answer is that it all depends on the condition of the individual. 'Condition' means not simply or necessarily the result of experience. There

are days when even the most experienced practi-
tioner of the art of prayer finds that all he can manage is a simple form of words, possibly his own,
possibly some well-known text which has become
soaked in his own associations. There may be days
when he feels that he can hardly be said to mean
what he is saying. At best, by a willed effort, he
means to mean it. The words of the psalm, 'I have
become like a dumb animal in your presence' (Ps.
73.22) may best express what he is feeling, or not
feeling.

For one of the problems about praying is that we
have to learn to be independent of feeling. Some
days, for whatever reason, we go to pray readily and
almost eagerly. There are others on which we can
bring ourselves to pray only with the greatest effort
of the will. Perhaps for most people, most of the
time, it becomes a matter of routine. This is why
it is important to develop a habit of praying, daily,
if possible at fixed time, or at least for a fixed time.
No matter how busy we are we can all manage to
find time to read the paper, to listen to or watch
the news on radio or television. We tell ourselves
that it is important to keep up with what is going
on. This is quite true. It is important. But is it more
important than being able to put that news into a
larger context? How often do we not find that the
latest news bulletin has a depressing effect, unless
we are braced to meet it by seeing it *sub specie
aeternitatis*, in the long perspective of the mind of
God. Not that this makes us insensitive to the
spectacle of human suffering. On the contrary.
But it does mean that we can, for example, relate
that suffering to the never-ending achievement of

Christ's redemptive suffering. We can see it as truly a suffering of the body of Christ, the royal road of the cross that leads to final triumph. Nor is this mere escapism. As Thomas Merton says:

> A contemplative will concern himself with the same problems as other people, but he will try to get to the spiritual and metaphysical roots of these problems—not by analysis but by simplicity.

Or, as Monica Furlong puts it:

> Contemplation can only result from a sense that one has coped courageously with one's environment and with one's inner problems; it is not an escape from successful activity but a development from it. It is this which gives prayer its meaning and integrity. (*Contemplating Now*, p. 74)

In other words, prayer, true prayer, is an important element in any genuine human life. To neglect it, to be 'too busy' for it, is to exclude a factor, *the* factor, which will help me to become more fully myself and therefore more fully capable of entering into the concerns of others. For the effect of prayer is to root myself more and more consciously in the very ground of my being, which is the ground of all being, the ground on which I am united with all my fellow-men, where I can truly 'identify' with them.

It may seem surprising that, immediately after describing a situation in which we may be capable of no more than a very simple form of vocal prayer, we should go on to talk of contemplation, which we tend to regard as the prerogative of a minority of people, chiefly to be found amongst members of religious orders who have shut themselves off from 'the world' in order to devote themselves more or less exclusively to God and the thought of the 'next' world. But, as Merton himself says in the passage we have just quoted:

> if a monk is permitted to be detached from these struggles over particular interests, it is only in order that he may give more thought to the interests of all, to the whole question of the re-conciliation of all men with one another in Christ.

What needs to be re-emphasised for the rest of us, in the context of our present discussion, is that in any form of prayer, from the utterance of the simplest prayer-formula or personal conversation with God right up to the mystical experiences of the great geniuses of the art, one common thread unites them all. It will help to elucidate the meaning of this statement if we look at a familiar definition of prayer as 'the raising of the mind and heart to God'. The words 'mind and heart' must be seen as summing up the wholeness of man. We are intelligent, truth-seeking creatures. We are, at the same time, loving creatures, able to 'give our hearts' to what we see to be good, to desire that good for what it is. In a not uncommon response, our desire is a selfish desire, the longing to possess. But the real thing, true love, desires that that which is loved shall go on being what it is. The true lover wishes not so much to get as to give.

We have already seen that such love is the central reality, the ultimate truth at the very core of creation. In the exercise of prayer, in raising or opening our minds and hearts to God, we come to see this as a dazzling truth; but, still more, we respond to this truth in a way that goes beyond any merely intellectual recognition. The artist's response to a beautiful landscape is not a cold appraisal of planes and tones and patterns. It is a desire to perpetuate that beauty in his painting. Obviously, the intellectual element, the recognition of the qualities that go to make up the whole scene, is an essential part of his appreciation. But a sophisticated computer might be programmed to enumerate and co-ordinate such qualities. What makes a man an artist is the ability to put his technical skill at the service of an inspiration which is the outcome of a passionate and intense appreciation. In the same way, what we call 'raising the heart' to God is immeasurably more than a cold intellectual response to a metaphysical proposition. Theologians are not necessarily better men or better Christians because they can discourse learnedly about the nature of God. Intellectual recognition does not, of itself, stir to action, or even evoke more than a tepid response.

But how, in fact, do we so raise our hearts to God? Here we are faced with the paradoxical situation summed up in Pascal's famous aphorism: 'You would not be looking for me if you had not already found me.' Are we up against a blank wall of mystification? Is it possible to analyse the situation a little further, to cast some light on this puzzle? The answer is to be found in the situation we have already looked at, the nature of God and man's relation to him. In the words of Monica Furlong:

'Atheist, agnostic, or believer in one religion or another, godseeking is built unto us' (*Contemplating Now*, p. 12). Although most agnostics would deny this roundly, the fact remains that all men are committed to a seeking beyond themselves. Even the simplest sort of curiosity, to say nothing of the quest of the philosopher or the scientist, testifies to man's desire to know. The attraction which beauty in one shape or another exercises upon us all is another indication that we need to find beyond ourselves a satisfaction which we do not find within. The fact that no man can do without friendship of some sort unless, as Aristotle says, 'he is either a beast or a god', similarly proves that need for what Rahner calls 'self-transcendence'. The solipsist is mad: the narcissist is, to say the least, abnormal—though we all have some of the qualities of each of them.

Now, if it is true that God is indeed the Answer to every possible question; if he is the sheer Beauty that is fragmented for us in a million beautiful sights or objects; if he is the Love which is uttered stammeringly in any human love; it follows that, in some sense, however limited, we have already found him in the small discoveries we make, the moments of beauty we experience, the love that we enjoy, however fleetingly. All too many of us think to continue the search at the same level exclusively, pursuing our scientific researches, adding to our moments of aesthetic pleasure, plunging more and more deeply into the same sort of social (or sexual) round. But, as C. S. Lewis brings out so well in *Pilgrim's Regress,* at that level final satisfaction never comes. Or, in St Augustine's statement, 'we are made with a bias in our natures towards you, Lord, and our hearts are restless until they come to rest in you'.

So it is important to insist that the quest for God is not just another stage in man's intellectual, aesthetic, amorous adventure. It is precisely in the dissatisfaction we felt with these pursuits that the divine invitation presents itself. 'The world is charged with the grandeur of God.' But to identify the world's beauty with the divine grandeur is to bring the Creator down to the level of his creation. It is like identifying a performance of a symphony with its composer, like failing to distinguish between the characters in a Shakespearean play and the playwright himself. For whilst it is true that, as Simon Weil has said, 'it is only through things and individual beings on earth that human love can penetrate to what lies beyond', it is precisely what lies beyond which is the object of our search. Teilhard de Chardin expresses this aspect of our study in these words:

Sometimes people think that they can increase your attraction in my eyes by stressing almost exclusively the charm and goodness of your human life in the past. But truly, O Lord, if I wanted to cherish only a man, then I would surely turn to those whom you have given me in the allurements of their present flowering. Are there not, with our mothers, brothers, friends and sisters, enough irresistibly lovable people around us? Why should we turn to Judaea two thousand years ago? No, what I cry out for, like every being, with my whole life and all my earthly passion, is something very different from an equal to cherish: it is a God to adore.

To adore ... that means to lose oneself in the unfathomable, to plunge into the inexhaustible, to find peace in the incorruptible, to be absorbed in defined immensity, to offer oneself to the fire and the transparency, to annihilate oneself in proportion as one becomes more deliberately conscious of oneself, and to give of oneself, and to give of one's deepest to that whose depth has no end.... The more man becomes man, the more will he become prey to a need, a need that is always more explicit, more subtle and more magnificent, the need to adore. (*Milieu Divin*, pp. 127–8)

The language of adoration has become debased by so much of our modern usage. People 'adore' their favourite chocolate, pop-star, composer. When a young man says to a young woman 'I adore you', he is at least expressing a certain sense of awe in the presence of a power that exercises sway over him. But even this experience is pallid indeed in comparison with the sense of utter prostration in the presence of what von Hugel call the 'stupendously rich Reality' of God.

Yet the paradox at the heart of the prayer-experience is that it requires of us both a total surrender of all desire for that which we adore and at the same time a recognition of its total desirableness. We adore God, we sink down in a wordless attitude of praise and thankfulness that the ultimate truth about the universe is that, under all its limitation and frustration and ugliness and horror, there is, concealed yet known to our inner eye, this total Goodness and Beauty and Majesty and Power. And because this final Reality is also the sheer power of enriching love that seeks to give and give and give, we see too that our response must be also a willingness to receive. Otherwise the divine Love itself would be frustrated. But our willingness to receive becomes a totally selfless readiness to co-operate with the selflessness of God. The closer we come to the still centre where the love of God is concentrated, the more shall we ourselves begin to approximate at least in intention and hope to the total self-dedication that is the essence of the Christian way of life.

For most of us, most of the time—possibly all the time—such language remains all but meaningless. Yet we have the assurance of the great heroes of this Way that, in the final stages of the ascent to God, there is brought about the sort of fusion which takes place when the metal is plunged into the furnace, to take upon itself the intensity of heat which the furnace itself is, but which is communicated to the metal, so that it is as though the latter had been absorbed into the former. But the metal has not disappeared. It remains itself, purged of all that is not metal, every kind of dross or impurity, so that it can be said to have taken on the qualities of fire. It can communicate to others the warmth and the light which the fire has engendered in it.

Those who think, as many do think, that the practice of contemplative prayer is essentially a self-seeking desire to become 'good', have totally misunderstood the situation. There are indeed those who seem to think that the Christian way is no more than a kind of spiritual callisthenics, building the soul beautiful rather than the body beautiful. But unless their spiritual exercises burn out all egoism until they cease to be interested in their own spiritual state, except in so far as they must regret anything that impedes their effective response to the divine summons, they have scarcely begun to understand the call of Christ. Nor is it right to think of prayer as primarily inspired by a curiosity about God, a desire to 'understand' him better. Returning to our analogy with the composer or playwright who is 'behind' his productions, it is clear that we are not particularly helped to appreciate Beethoven's music by knowing that he was deaf, nor does information about the notorious 'second-best bed' bequeathed to Anne Hathaway tell us anything about the problem of Hamlet's madness or the identity of the Dark Lady of the Sonnets. Thus, theological talk about God is not only unhelpful; it can be positively distracting, just as a study of Freud or Jung is by no means the best introduction to the experience of falling in love. Indeed we have to be detached from the desire for any kind of intellectual satisfaction if we are to arrive at that goal where imagery, thought, desire are all unheeded. We are no longer concerned with what the poet calls:

> the intolerable wrestle
> with words and meanings.

'Be still'—emotionally, imaginatively, intellectually —and yet somehow 'know that I am God'.

To sum up what may seem to be a rather untidy and ill-organised chapter, we begin with the reminder that prayer should be seen as the personal response of this unique individual to a Being whose very freedom from all limitation entails the fact that his is no generalised benevolence. He has established a relationship between each individual creature and himself that is unique. Since prayer is the explicit recognition of that relationship, it follows that the prayer of any human being must be peculiar to that individual and to no other. 'Progress' in prayer means, therefore, developing a more and more personal awareness of the meaning of God to *me* and to no other. Even if we begin, as most of us do begin, with traditional formulas of one sort or another, we do not begin to pray in any real sense of the word until we have made those formulas our own, realising their associations for me in my situation. For example if, in reciting a psalm, I am thinking of the circumstances in which it was composed, what it meant to David or some other composer, this is at best what we can only call a second-hand sort of prayer. And the sooner we are able to practise some form of 'mental prayer' or meditation, even it may be alongside our vocal prayer, the better. If the time comes when we find this to be unrewarding, we should not hesitate to move on to a more simplified form of prayer, the beginning of contemplation, resting in the thought of God—God's unchangeableness, stillness, peace, absolute goodness, wisdom, knowledge ... the attitude which is summed up in the familiar text: 'Be still and know that I am God.' This may or may not be accompanied by any felt satisfaction. Sooner or later, feelings will be seen to be irrelevant either way. One is filled with an unformulated yet genuine urge for God. One's own success, even 'success' in prayer, becomes less and less significant. Again, in Dante's famous line: 'In his will is our peace.' At every stage the golden rule is that formulated by Chapman: 'Pray as you can and do not try to pray as you can't.'

One grows too in a recognition of the mysteriousness, in a sense the unpredictability, of God. He is, of course, only unpredictable in the sense that he does not always do the things that we *expect* him to do. The sooner we stop expecting the better. All we know, all we can possibly know, is what is here and now. At the same time we do know what this here and now means, not only in the matter of my relationship to God, but also in all that concerns my fellow-men. For, as we have thought, growing in an awareness of God as the very ground of my being means that I now also grow in a realisation that he is the ground of all that is, and therefore of all other human beings. Aware as I am of my own importance in his eyes, I equally come to see that the importance of all others to him is no less real. The practical consequences of this idea need no further development.

2

THE PRAYER OF JESUS

In thinking about our own experience of prayer, we saw that, whilst it is in one sense an activity we share with countless others, it is at the same time supremely personal and individual. When, therefore, we turn to reflect on the prayer of Jesus himself, we need to stress this element of uniqueness in a very special way. For, whilst it is true that he is 'like us in everything, except sin', his humanity is marked out from that of all other men by the fact of the utterly unparalleled relationship existing between that humanity and the very Godhead.

How then dare we presume to suppose that anything we have to say in this matter can in any way express the mystery of that ineffable relationship? Clearly, we do not suggest that it is possible for anybody to understand, still less to describe, what that relationship must have been like. At the same time we need to emphasise a truth which has often been lost sight of, out of a mistaken effort to safeguard our reverence for the divine element in the total personality of one who—remaining in a special sense Son of God—was yet in the habit of speaking of himself as Son of Man. We can best appreciate the meaningfulness of the Incarnation by always bearing in mind the truth that the Father is revealed in and through the human activities, ideas, emotions, words and outlook of one who lived out his life within a defined historical period, in a specific cultural and social setting, inheriting a religious tradition which was unlike any other. If he moulded that tradition he was able so to mould it precisely because he was this individual and not another; judging it with his unique capacity for judging; evaluating it in the light of the ideals he had developed as the outcome of an interplay between what he had received and what he had himself discovered.

We have much evidence to enable us to indicate the sort of influences that went to the shaping of what we may call his spiritual development. The evidence is derived not primarily from the gospels but from the literature that was already in existence in his own day; and from sources that have come to us through non-Christian authorities and which therefore cannot be said to have been modified by later Christian theologising. It is only after we have looked at the influences that controlled the development of the qualities of his mind and heart that we shall turn to think of the way in which such influences were reflected in the teaching that has been attributed to him.

His psychological development—a term we must use for want of a better—may be seen at two levels. On the one hand, the maturing of his human psyche, his intellectual, moral and emotional growth, was conditioned by factors common to human beings in general, even whilst their effect is to enable a human being to be this unique individual and no other. Family influences, of course;

all that network of relationships which are necessary for the achievement of a balanced temperament; a growing awareness of what it meant to be not just himself, Jesus of Nazareth, but himself as a Jew, proud of his race, conscious of the great historical and religious heritage which he shared with his fellow-Jews; a realisation of the complex political situation in which his country was involved; a deepening understanding of the different religious groups working to affect, perhaps to contaminate, the purity of the divine revelation.

In a brutal age he yet developed a great sensitivity to human suffering; in an increasingly sophisticated age he ever maintained a simplicity of outlook, an insistence on the fundamental values of a genuinely human existence. To some extent this was due to the fact that he had been reared in the simplicities of village life in a village that was unknown and unregarded. But he was and remained unspoilt because of some interior quality which enabled him to meet every sort of human being—wealthy Pharisee, learned scholar, public official, social outcast—and remain himself, poised, self-possessed, tolerant of everything except what touched his Father's honour.

For—and here we enter on the second level of his growth to the fulness of manhood—along with his increasing awareness of the world about him went a still deeper realisation of the inner world of the spirit. At the beginning of his public mission, we are told that he spent 'forty days', a not inconsiderable period of time, in solitude; a kind of spiritual preparation for his future work. During the crowded months of preaching and healing he would spend nights in prayer. Throughout his teaching he insisted constantly on the central importance of prayer. On the eve of his death he turned to prayer in the garden 'as his custom was'. It is impossible not to conclude that all this was a development and a continuation of an earlier practice. All that we have said above about the experience of prayer applies to Jesus, though to a degree which is incalculable. Yet even he must have learnt how to pray.

In the psychological–spiritual development of any human being, not excluding the Son of God, it is impossible to exaggerate the importance of that network of human relationships to which we have already referred. The child's earliest consciousness is stimulated by those physical feelings, those sounds and sights about him, which constitute the subject-matter of his experience. He is presumably more aware of them than of 'himself' except in the sense that he can 'experience' them only because of their relationship to his own sense-awareness. This child is more conscious of what he feels, hears, sees than of the fact that it is he who is so affected. It is only at a later stage of sophisticated self-awareness that I begin to analyse these sensations as *my* sensations, to develop a consciousness of myself as this self, over against other selves.

For Jesus, the first experiences were experiences of his mother's body—warm, soft, protecting. And since it is pretty certain that he spent the greater part of his life in her company, it follows that, from those earliest sensations to the final sight of her on Calvary, she remained the major single influence in his total human development. Even though it has become fashionable for scholars to speak of the infancy narratives in Matthew and Luke as largely legendary, it would be crassly insensitive to refuse to believe that there was in Mary of Nazareth a remarkable quality of spiritual perceptiveness. Equally unjustified would be a failure to recognise the bond of profound sympathy that existed between this particular son and this mother.

At the very least we must see Mary as not inferior to the great women-prototypes in the Bible. If she did not describe herself as 'handmaid of the Lord', it is significant that whatever 'source' Luke may have used did in fact ascribe these words to her. If she did not herself utter the *Magnificat*, we find it difficult not to believe that it represented her mind; that its biblical echoes were consciously present to her during the months during which she was waiting for the birth of her child. All this is no more than a claim that Mary's attitude was at the very least that of many another Jewish woman in her situation. Nourished on the Bible, she was able to introduce her son to its riches when the time came.

It was she who taught him his first prayers, communicated something of her own spirit. With Esther he could say:

'I have been taught from my earliest years, in the bosom of my family, that you, Lord, chose Israel out of all the nations, and our ancestors out of all the people of old times, to be your heritage for ever.' (Esth. 4.17)

One of the remarkable characteristics of the Jewish people is the way in which family life and the larger life of the community as a whole are

49

blended into a homogeneous experience. For there is a sense in which the nation is truly the family writ large. The general framework of Jewish religious observance has changed astonishingly little down the centuries, so that we can speak with confidence of the general background to the personal experience of Jesus during his early years. The infusion of prayer into the daily round was supported by the regular synagogue services, the weekly Sabbath observance, the annual festivals: Passover and Shavuos ('weeks', Hellenised into 'Pentecost'); Tabernacles, with its outdoor huts and waving palms; Yom Kippur, the great Day of Atonement on which the high priest, in the name of the whole people, sought forgiveness for his and their transgressions of the Law; Purim, a sort of carnival celebrating the deliverance of the Jews from the machinations of Hamar; Hanuka, the festival of lights, recalling the great achievement of the Maccabaean revolt. The relationship of the Jewish nation in all its activities to the One God was inescapable. And, as Herman Wouk says:

No other nation ever undertook as a matter of law, to love God, to observe his commandments, to love their neighbours as themselves, to protect widows and orphans, to feed and clothe the poor....

Within this larger framework, the more detailed observance of a devout Jewish family had its more continuous influence, with its morning and evening prayer, continual thanksgiving to God, King of the Universe, who brings forth bread from the earth, who is the creator of the fruit of the vine, of light, of life itself. The whole of the daily round was shot through with the consciousness of the ever-present activity of God, with whom man was called to collaborate in the fulfilment of creation. When we are told in the fourth gospel that on one occasion Jesus said, in reply to a charge of breaking the Sabbath, 'my Father goes on working and so do I' (John 5.17), we recognise a thought that was ever present to his mind as he plied his trade as a carpenter during those long years at Nazareth. This particular piece of wood, this present task, was his opportunity to continue the divine creativity. 'He who sent me is with me, and has not left me to myself, for I always do what pleases him' (John 8.29) is another echo of the truth he had come to appreciate during the time of his maturing.

But all this he can be said to have shared with any devout Jewish workman. What is there to be said about the nature of his spirituality, his prayer-life, which was peculiar to him alone, as this individual and no other? Here, of course, speculation must be tentative, hesitant and totally provisional. It is impossible for us to be certain about the thought-processes of another human being, even a contemporary, even a loved one. More difficult, then, to be at all positive in seeking to enter into the mind of someone living in a distant age. Supremely difficult to feel any sort of confidence about the sort of suggestion that follows. Yet, for reasons we have already seen, there is every reason why we should feel confident that we can know something and conscious that we should.

We believe then that, in a unique sense, 'God was in Christ', that he and the Father constituted one reality, that in seeing him his followers saw the Father. These are expressions of an idea that became more and more explicit in the Church until Nicaea and Chalcedon formally defined the relationship as one of two natures in one person. Now, unless this development was a complete falsification of the truth, we are driven to believe that it means that Jesus himself must have been at least dimly aware that he was not like other men. It requires very little introspective self-awareness to come to a realisation of one's unique loneliness. Every man *is*, in one sense, an island, sundered from every other man in his unshared individuality. Who am I? What am I? These are questions that thrust themselves upon us.

Here, of course, we are at the very heart of the problem of the spirituality of Jesus. In our analysis of what prayer means to us ordinary mortals, we stressed the basic truth that it enables the human entity, body–soul, to be somehow aware of its total dependence on God, coupled with a realisation that that dependence does not mean passivity or lack of responsibility. On the contrary, the very openness of God means that the power of God flows more and more unimpeded into and through his human agent. Now if it is possible for this to be experienced by us, it was certainly experienced in a unique way by Jesus. In his developing prayer he came to see more and more clearly that he was what he was as a human being only and utterly because in him the power of the Godhead had found its most perfect vehicle. If Paul could write those majestic passages in his letters to the Ephesians and the Colossians: 'He is the first-born of all creation, for in him all things were created in heaven and on earth'; 'all things were created through him'; 'he is before all things and in him all things hold together'; 'all things are summed up in Christ'; 'he is the image of the unseen God'—if such ideas were present to the mind of Paul, can we doubt that they were present also to the mind of Jesus? Present, it may be, in a wordless and inexplicit way, because his human mind needed time to assimilate and formulate them. All the mystics are agreed that what they come to know in the intimacy of their ecstatic union is literally ineffable and indescribable. It can only be filtered through the totally inadequate medium of human concepts and human language. For, as Newman says: 'What is language but an artificial system adapted for particular purposes, which have been determined by our wants?' Or in the words of T. S. Eliot: 'Last year's words belong to last year's language and next year's words await another voice.' So the mind of Jesus was limited in its workings by the fact that it had been developed within the context of the Jewish experience, conditioned by the Hebrew language.

But deeper still as his self-consciousness grew and matured, he came to a realisation of the radical unity that existed between himself and 'the Father'. This idea has become a theme for argument between different schools of theologians and biblical scholars. Some have argued that, since his references to the relationship between himself and the Father almost invariably seem to be formulated in ambiguous terms, this must mean that he was not sufficiently certain in his own mind about this truth. Others, arguing from what we may call *a priori* grounds, have said that, since he was divine, the consciousness of divinity must have been present to him from the beginning. But this is another example of a common error committed by theologians —the failure to remember that the material of their trade is something profoundly mysterious. Their efforts to understand and therefore to formulate are bound to be frustrated. The best they can do is to indicate the lines of a solution, bearing always in mind the fact that what they say refers only to one aspect of the surface of unplumbed depths.

So, in the present case, we must recognise that the mere fact that Jesus 'knew that he was God' does not mean that therefore his finite human intellect was capable of taking in what this *meant*. Even when he said, for example, 'the Father and I constitute one reality' or 'he who sees me sees the Father', we should not conclude that he necessarily appreciated the full implications of his words. An important element, perhaps the most important, in his prayer-life was that he was always growing in an appreciation of the truth about himself. After all, even we lesser mortals are constantly making discoveries about ourselves, realising more and more (though not necessarily more and more clearly) what it means to be 'me'. To suppose that, 'because he knew that he was God', he was therefore free of the struggles, the insecurities, the questionings, the fears, the loneliness, that are part of the human lot, is, in effect, to undermine the truth of the Incarnation. He was *human*; the Word was made *flesh*; he was made *like us*. In a famous passage, which can never be too much studied, von Hugel says:

If there is nothing shifting or fitful or simply changing about him, there is everywhere energy and expansion, thought and emotion, effort and experience, joy and sorrow, loneliness and conflict, interior trial and triumph, exterior defeat and supplantation: particular affections, particular humiliations, homely labour, a homely heroism, greatness throughout in littleness. (*Mystical Element*, I, 26)

In other words, even for him, prayer was a continuing discovery. To the end of his days, he was learning ever more about the nature of the ground of his being. He was probing ever more deeply into the reality which has been the object of man's worship, man's aspirations, man's contemplation from the beginning of his religious history. The great mystics, as we know, have arrived at what they seem to feel as a fusion of their personalities with the divine personality, a fusion in which they cease somehow to be themselves and yet, in losing what Merton calls their 'empirical self'—the self which is earthbound, restricted to the here and now, at the mercy of the chances and changes of this mortal life—they discover a deeper and more authentic self, the reality which lies behind and is concealed by the superficial experiences of day-to-day living. At this level, they achieve a unity with God, based, it would seem, on the realisation that whatever they have and are is both a 'given', distinguishing them from God, and is also a participation by grace in the divine nature itself. In the case of Jesus we must suppose that what he discovered was that at the human level the 'given' was a kind of reflection of the transcendental unity which, in theological terms, binds together the three several persons of the Trinity. Yet, as we have thought, the mere attempt to put these mysteries into words inevitably distorts them. All we can do is to confess our incomprehension whilst believing that some dim indication of the truth lies behind the traditional formulas to which we subscribe.

One thing of which we can be certain is that, at the same time, he was strengthening his natural conviction of his solidarity with his fellow-men. In a remarkable passage, Herman Wouk has this to say:

> All the prophecy of Israel turns on one simple but extremely difficult idea; namely that *all Israel, living and dead, from Sinai to the present hour stands in its relation to God as a single immortal individual.* ... The immortal individual who entered the Covenant still lives. On days of annual judgement and atonement, this individual strikes the balance of his performance under the Covenant and confesses his failures.

The Covenant had bound the Jewish individual–nation to God in a unique way. The chosen people were called to a redemptive destiny. 'I will make you the light of the nations so that my salvation may reach to the ends of the earth' (Isa. 49.6). It was the sort of text to fire the imagination and inspire the heart of men less spiritually perceptive than Jesus. It filled him with a desire to share in that work of salvation. In the prayer with which the fourth gospel concludes the account of the Last Supper, Jesus is quoted as saying: 'for their sake I consecrate myself, so that they too may be consecrated in truth' (John 17.19). But this was no new prayer. It had been the driving-force of his whole mission.

What precisely 'salvation' meant was something which he would learn to understand more fully only as the years passed. From his early years, until he finally left Nazareth for his life of preaching, he saw it as much in terms of deliverance from oppression, suffering, enslavement as deliverance from sin and other spiritual ills. In the Jewish tradition the physical was so often correlated with the spiritual, poverty and political subjection seen as the punishment of infidelity, that deliverance from the former became almost a symbol of spiritual liberation, if not actually conditioned by it. In at least two of the miracle-stories recorded in the gospels, the link between sin and suffering is explicitly mentioned (John 5.14; 9.20), whilst two disasters are quoted (Luke 13.2,4) as exemplifying the same principle: 'Unless you repent you will all perish as they did.' It is significant that the passage which Jesus read in the synagogue at Nazareth (according to Luke 4.18) describes the 'good news' in terms of liberation and restoring sight to the blind. No doubt these passages can and should be interpreted in a metaphorical sense. Yet the lesson of his life as his later followers saw it was that 'salvation' was no purely spiritual achievement. It included the physical and material as well.

However he envisaged such salvation, he came increasingly to believe that he was to be in some special way God's instrument for its realisation. Reflecting on the history of his nation, he thought of the great men and women, from Moses to the

Maccabees, who had delivered the Jews from the oppressor, the invader, the persecutor. As he read or listened to the ninth chapter of Isaiah, telling of the humiliation of Zebulun in which his own village lay, he would have been insensitive indeed had he not related the passage to the present situation. His Galilee was now ruled over by the Idumaean fox, Herod Antipas, whose authority was in turn subject to the smile or frown of the Roman Emperor. Judaea, including the ancient kingdom of Judah, in which lay the Holy City itself, was taken over by the Romans in the year A.D. 6, possibly the very year when Jesus, at the age of twelve, is said to have gone up to Jerusalem for the Passover festival.

Already, in the years following his birth, revolts had broken out on the death of Herod the Great, led by men who themselves aspired to kingship. To what extent their pretensions were inspired by messianic notions is uncertain, though both Josephus the Jew and Tacitus the Roman historian refer to contemporary messianic expectations. The influence of such happenings on the development of the mentality of Jesus would have been to turn his thoughts to the problem of messianic deliverance. Those who argue that he could never have thought of himself in such terms are surely forgetting how much these notions were in the air. If there is any historical foundation for the story of the discussion between Jesus and the doctors on the occasion of his visit to the Temple at the age of twelve, it may be suggested that one of the questions under discussion would be precisely the nature of the deliverance to come.

That his own mind was turning towards the notion of a divine kingdom 'not of this world' was an almost inevitable development. There are, of course, those who hold that Jesus was actually involved in the whole movement which sought to deliver the country from Roman rule by violent means. Their arguments are hardly convincing except to those who believe that the gospels were simply an elaborate propaganda exercise to cover up a discreditable story and to draw a picture of Jesus almost the exact opposite of the truth. They need not detain us here. If it were true that the 'second-generation Christians' were able to develop a teaching which was more 'spiritual', more 'unworldly', more universally loving than that of Jesus himself, this would mean that they were themselves on a higher plane of spirituality than he was. This is absurd.

Apart from anything else, the very failure of so many attempts to set up a 'kingdom' independent of Rome, the widespread 'brigandage' which accompanied such attempts, the brutal repression of them – on one occasion the Romans crucified two thousand rebels – drove him to ask whether there was not some other way of setting his people free. If God's promises meant anything, if Israel was to be the 'light of the nations' through whom salvation would reach the 'ends of the earth', there must be some other way of achieving this. Successive earthly monarchies had come and gone. The great days of David and Solomon had given way to the sad story of the divided kingdom; the Assyrian, Babylonian, Egyptian, Syrian and finally Roman domination. Whatever historical actuality lay behind the gospel story of the 'temptation' when Jesus was offered the kingdoms of the world by the Tempter on one condition, the spiritual truth it embodies is clear. He came to see that earthly power, earthly sovereignty, was somehow necessarily tainted with evil. Impossible that his Father's kingdom should be so tainted. It must be of a different nature.

His own contribution, then, to the fulfilment of his people's destiny must be to win them over to this new concept. After all, the survival of the Jews as a distinct nation was due in the end to their religious convictions, to their faith in the protecting and guiding hand of God. The various disasters which had befallen them had been the result of their spiritual failures. Therefore only a change of heart, a turning away from material hopes and dreams of military glory, would bring about the only success that really mattered. Prophet after prophet had taught the same sort of message. He must himself assume the same prophetic role.

Such, in broad outline and with full recognition of the tentative nature of our speculations, will have been something of the background to his development as this individual Jew, living at this particular moment in his country's history. Any appreciation of his prayer-life needs to be rooted in some appreciation of the actual situation in which he lived. No human being comes to maturity in isolation from his fellows and from their concerns. No authentic spirituality can be divorced from the human context. In the words of Thomas Merton:

> I must look for my identity somehow not only in God but in other men.

I will never be able to find myself if I isolate myself from the rest of mankind as if I were a different kind of being. (*Seeds of Contemplation*, p. 20)

It is not surprising then that the proclamation of the coming kingdom was prefaced by a call to 'repentance', to a radical change of attitude, a turning away from former ideas and practices to a new faith and a new hope. 'The kingdom of God is close at hand. Repent, and believe the good news' (Mark 1.15). Already he is pictured as having submitted himself to John's baptism in an act of public repentance. It was a gesture which the Baptist is portrayed as wishing to resist. But, as Jesus replied, it was 'fitting that we should, in this way, do all that righteousness demands' (Matt. 3.15). Whatever his own personal sinlessness may have been, he could not 'isolate himself from the rest of mankind as if he were a different kind of being'. As on Yom Kippur, the day of 'annual judgement and atonement', the nation–individual was confessing its failures. He was associating himself with that confession.

He was associating himself with that confession because, during the long years of preparation at Nazareth, he had come to recognise the nature of his and his Father's involvement with his fellowmen. In thinking of our own experience of prayer, we have seen that it enables us to realise more and more effectively the truth that at the heart of reality is the ever-energising divine self-giving which is the explanation of the existence of all created being. Each of us comes to accept, with greater or less conviction, the basic fact of a relationship between the individual self and the Selfhood of God, a relationship of total dependence on our side, of total generosity on the other. The mutual self-giving which establishes the triune Godhead itself is reflected in the creative self-giving *ad extra,* 'beyond' the life of the Trinity. Since, then, creation depends on its Creator, the Creator is necessarily involved in that creative process. Jesus therefore came to see himself as the supreme expression of the creative *fiat*—'let us make man in our own image'—to see himself, as we have thought, as the perfect manifestation in human terms of the divine act of generation 'begetting' the Son. Yet, as Son and Father are also one, their mutual involvement is total. Not such is the involvement of the Creator with his creatures. Nevertheless somehow, mysteriously, inexpressibly, incomprehensibly, there must be some genuine involvement, if we are to believe that 'God's love for us was revealed when God sent into the world his only Son' (1 John 4.9). But—and here we are back at the very centre of our problem—how can we envisage the mysterious relationship between Jesus of Nazareth, this man at this point in the history of the world, and the time–space-transcending Being whom we call the Word, the Son 'begotten of the Father before all ages'?

Once again we must recall that we are in the face of mystery, of a situation which we believe to be the case but which we are unable to comprehend. In a sense it is analogous to the mystery of the Trinity. One thing that is absolutely certain about God is that he is One. In so far as philosophy can help, it encourages us to see that, since infinity cannot be multiplied, the Infinite Being we call God must be single. The Shema, the great affirmation uttered daily by every Jew, and therefore deep in the heart of Jesus, declared: 'Hear, O Israel, the Lord our God is the One God (Deut. 6.4). This great monotheistic faith has been accepted both by Christian and Muslim alike. Whatever, therefore, is meant by the 'Trinity', it cannot in any way impair or blemish the single simplicity that God is. In the same way, whatever the traditional formula about 'two natures in one person' may mean, it cannot mean and must not be taken to mean that there is any duality within the being that he is. In speaking of the 'search for God' which is the essential movement of prayer, we quoted Pascal's words: 'You would not be looking for me if you had not already found me.' We must surely believe of Jesus that he had always already found and did not need to seek.

And yet, if he really was made 'like us in everything but sin', there must be something in his experience which reflects the search and the struggle in which we lesser mortals are involved. Possibly an analogy with creation may help. God, we believe, is all-powerful, in the sense that he is the fulness of power, that there is no power at all that does not originate with him. In choosing to create he has chosen to call into being forces which are, in a real sense, independent of him. Were that not so, there could be no evil in the world. He would always be in a position to override the wrong choices of his human creatures, to intervene to control the waywardness of natural forces. But this would be to diminish the dignity of his creatures, to make them automata, puppets dangling from a string. But no;

they have their independence, even if that independence is his gift to them.

In the same sort of way, dare we suggest that the 'created aspect' of the Uncreated Son, the audible expression of the eternal divine Word has been given its own independent reality. True, the analogy breaks down, as all analogies do, because the distinction between God as Creator and the rest of creation does constitute a real duality, whereas the distinction between God and Christ is, as we have suggested, like the distinction between the three Persons of the Trinity, a distinction which yet does not divide them.

Many a modern theologian would, of course, dissent from any such interpretation. For them Jesus, coming into the world like any other human being, became somehow a God-possessed man. His human nature was taken over, by being absorbed into the divinity. What we are suggesting is that, with Scotus, we must see the Incarnation as the crowning work of creation. God who 'gave himself' in his creative act, as the musician 'puts himself' into his composition, in a final outpouring of love, emptied himself, in Paul's dramatic phrase, so that he not merely looked like a human being; he actually became one.

What does this *mean*? We have suggested above that this is not just our problem. It was a problem for Jesus himself. In his prayer-experience, he strove, as the great mystics have striven, to pierce through the veil of his 'empirical self', to become ever more aware of the true ground of his being, that Godhead with whom he knew himself to be united inseparably, whilst the very circumstances of his day-to-day living seemed to obscure what he 'knew'. The effect of his contemplative activity was two-fold. It helped him to deepen to an increasing extent the awareness he had of the Transcendent–Immanent. Not that such an awareness could be reduced to conceptual or propositional formulation. Here, we must repeat, Jesus was limited as the mystics are, seeing yet unable to state what is seen. The other effect was to enlarge his sympathy with all who shared his human limitations. But, if it was not possible to formulate to himself at all adequately the truth about himself, how could he hope to explain to others the truth which he had glimpsed? Professor Mascall, in his Christological study, has suggested that Jesus deliberately 'talked down', as it were, to his disciples; expressing ideas which were clear enough to him in ways that brought these ideas down to the level of their comprehension. Yet the truth would seem to be that he could not adequately clarify his ideas even to himself.

An example of the sort of experience which he may have had is to be found in the story of the Transfiguration. The fact that this incident is described in all three synoptists persuades most critics that it is based on some actual historical event. The presence of Moses and Elijah is taken as a symbolic expression of the idea that, in Jesus, Law and Prophecy have found their fulfilment. It may have another meaning too. It may well mean that, in such experiences, Jesus is temporarily freed from the limitations of time and space. The fact that the three disciples are described as sharing in the experience may be taken as symbolic of the way in which Jesus himself came to appreciate the power that was in him, the power to raise others up to his level, to enable others to share in his experiences, his vision. As the author of the Second Letter of Peter says:

We brought you the knowledge and the coming of our Lord Jesus Christ; we had seen his majesty for ourselves. He was honoured and glorified by God the Father, when the Sublime Glory spoke to him and said: this is my Son, the Beloved, he enjoys my favour. We heard this ourselves, spoken from heaven, when we were with him on the holy mountain. (1.16–18)

The apostles 'heard' indeed. But we can be quite sure that the experience could not be translated into meaningful terms until, after the Resurrection, the staggering truth became apparent to them. The Sublime Glory, the Shekinah, the bright Presence of God, traditionally dwelling in the Holy of Holies, itself a permanent continuation of the Tent of Meeting (Exod. 40.34; 1 Kgs. 8.11), was dwelling in this man. The fact that John, too, without referring definitely to the Transfiguration, speaks of seeing 'his glory', indicates how great an impression this incident had made.

But what has this to do with the prayer-life of our Lord? Simply this: that it relates the experience of Jesus to similar experiences recorded of the great mystics down the ages. Paul, we remember, 'heard things which must not and cannot be put into human language' having been 'caught up right into the third heaven' (2 Cor. 12.2,3). Again we remind ourselves of the human limitations accepted

66

by Jesus, so that he too would be incapable of putting into 'human language' the things that he 'saw' or 'heard'. It was not till after the Resurrection that he was finally freed of these human restrictions. Entering into the 'glory of God' meant that he was 'now' in that timeless, spaceless condition which is the condition of God's very being. In that condition, described in conventional terminology as 'being at the right hand of the Father', the full significance of his earthly career was clear to him. Hitherto, like the rest of us—though, of course, with an immensely greater perceptivity—his insight into spiritual truth, even the truth about himself, was limited by the fact that his human consciousness was controlled by its being linked to the material medium of brain and nervous system. The 'glorified state' of his post-Resurrection existence is the condition towards which all our spiritual striving is directed. When we are told that he said to the two disciples going to Emmaus:

> You foolish men! So slow to believe the full message of the prophets! Was it not ordained that the Christ should suffer and so enter into his glory? Then starting with Moses and going through all the prophets he explained to them the passages throughout the scriptures that were about himself. (Luke 24.25–7)

is it presumptuous to suggest that the full realisation of that message had come to him only in and through his own Resurrection-experience? Only three days earlier, on the cross, he had felt a sense of abandonment—'My God, why have you deserted me?'—which would have been incompatible with a

67

clear understanding of what his suffering meant. He too had to be tested. He too had to experience that interior struggle which the greatest saints have known. The saints have known it because they are 'fallen' like the rest of us; their nature has to be straightened like a piece of twisted metal (to use Aloysius Gonzaga's description of himself). We do not think of the humanity of Christ as 'fallen', Yet it did share in the creaturely condition which meant that, of itself, it was incomplete. Its completion could come about only through the action upon it of the Spirit of God, an action to which it was ever open, but an action that could not achieve its effect instantaneously.

4

THE PRAYERS OF JESUS

It is natural to begin our study of the different prayers of our Lord's which are quoted in the gospels with the 'Our Father', that summary of the Christian attitude to God and to his creation. But as an introduction to our treatment of that great pronouncement, it will be helpful to begin with some reflection on a brief passage which occurs both in Matthew and Luke.

I bless you, Father, Lord of heaven and of earth, for hiding these things from the learned and the clever and revealing them to mere children. (Luke 10.21; Matt. 11.25)

The words are a reminder that the practice of prayer is not an intellectual exercise, dependent for its success on a store of knowledge or dialectical skill. As someone once said: 'You may as well throw your brains down behind the door when you go to prayer.' If intellectual capacity gave people any sort of advantage in the Christian life, this would mean that those of inferior education or poorer mental gifts would have greater difficulty in entering the kingdom. Not only is this contrary to experience; it is also an idea against which Jesus himself was repeatedly protesting. Much of his polemic against the 'scribes and Pharisees' sprang from his rejection of such a notion. For them skill in the Law set them apart from the rest. For him, it was rather the outcast, the meek, the heavily burdened, the unostentatious who were welcome.

We shall, then, best come to an appreciation of the prayers which are recorded in the gospels if we suspend our scholarly questioning about whether or not these are the authentic expressions of the mind of Jesus. However they came to be formulated, we can at least recognise that they spring from a tradition which, as we thought earlier, must be traceably connected with the original Preacher of the Good News. Certainly they have all played their part in forming that Christian mind which is the mind of Christ. And if the 'mind of Christ' is not an extension and a development of the mind of Jesus we must surely feel free to depart from it. In the words of Gerhard Ebeling:

> Were it to be proved that christology had no basis in the historical Jesus, or even was a misinterpretation of Jesus, christology would be finished.

To that extent we are justified in using the gospel passages as we have them, without speculating about their sources. Not that our Christian practice does not have to be intelligent. This is why we must try to find an answer to the nagging questions which sometimes hinder our total commitment to the demands made on us by our faith. Some of these we shall be wrestling with in the following pages.

Our Father

Perhaps the most important truth which Jesus emphasised to his listeners during his public life was the notion of the Fatherhood of God. Not that this notion was not already present in the Jewish tradition. In the Exodus story, Moses is instructed to tell Pharaoh: 'This is what Yahweh says: "Israel is my first-born son"' (Exod. 4.22); and in the Deuteronomic Code, Moses is represented as saying: 'You are sons of Yahweh your God' (Deut. 14.1). In a well-known passage the prophet Hosea stresses the tenderness of the relationships:

> When Israel was a child I loved him,
>   and I called my son out of Egypt ...
> I myself taught Ephraim to walk,
>   I took them in my arms ...
> I was like someone who lifts an infant close
>   against his cheek. (Hos. 14.1ff)

So, too, Jeremiah:

> I had thought you would call me, My Father
> and would never cease to follow me. (Jer. 3.19)

In the psalms, the fatherhood of God is thought of as referring directly to the king, through whom the divine bounty enriched the people:

> He has told me, 'You are my son,
> today have I become your father'. (Ps. 2.7)

In one sense, then, it was no new truth that Jesus was revealing. He was doing no more than to re-assert, in the light of his own spiritual experience, a truth which had been lost to view with the increasing formalising and institutionalising of the Jewish religion. Again and again, the prophets had inveighed against the attitude of mind which thought that the mere performance of certain ritual acts was a sufficient discharge of all that God demanded.

> I am sick of holocausts of rams
>   and the fat of calves....
> Take your wrong-doing out of my sight.
>   Cease to do evil
> Learn to do good. (Isa. 1.11, 16)

is only one of many similar passages which might be quoted. What above all concerned Jesus was that the failure to appreciate the reality of his Father's love had two disastrous effects. First of all religion had become a burden rather than an inspiration; secondly men had lost sight of the fatherly care which looked after the birds of the air and the flowers of the field. They were worth more than many a sparrow, he said with some irony, yet they allowed themselves to worry about material concerns and were blind to the abiding love of their heavenly Father.

When, therefore, we ourselves recite this prayer, it is well that we should pause for as long as may be on the fundamental idea. In our treatment of the experience of prayer in general, we referred to the traditional practice of putting ourselves 'in the presence of God'. It may be said that here we are being invited by Jesus himself to put ourselves in mind of the fatherliness of him to whom we are addressing our prayer. What that 'fatherliness' implies is a complex of qualities. In the first place, it refers to the basic truth of our total dependence

on our heavenly father. Perhaps we may here inter-
pose the suggestion that this is the reason why our
Lord warns us elsewhere to 'call no one on earth
your father' (Matt. 23.9). For the only being to
whom this title can be addressed with complete
truth is God. All other fatherhood is derivative and
relative. Here we have an excellent example of the
way in which language can mislead. Normally,
when we use the term 'Father' in thinking of or
speaking to God, we all but inevitably transfer to
him such ideas as our experience of earthly fatherhood may have developed in us. Yet even the most
perfect of fathers still falls infinitely short of the
perfection to be found in the universal father of all
mankind. It is true that, in the providence of God,
we owe our existence to the generative activity of
an earthly parent. Yet this activity is, it may be
said, little more than a symbol of the ever-present
creative activity of the Being who not only renders
effective the whole process of procreation but,
through the continuing operation of the secondary
causes effective throughout the universe, continues
to give me whatever is necessary for the support of
my body and the development of my spiritual
powers.

More: 'The proof that you are sons is that God
has sent the Spirit of his Son into our hearts: the
Spirit that cries "Abba, Father"' (Gal. 4.6). We are
not merely endowed with existence by the initial
creative act of God. Had we been merely brought
into existence, we should have been in the condition described by Paul in his letter to the Romans:

From the beginning till now the whole of creation, as we know, has been groaning in one great act of giving birth; and not only creation, but all of us, we who possess the first fruits of the Spirit, we too groan inwardly as we wait for our bodies to be set free. (Rom. 8.22,23)

That deliverance comes to us through the redemptive work of the Son, who has enabled us to become sons of his Father and co-heirs with him in the glory that is now his, into which we too shall enter. For what has happened is that we have not merely come into our natural existence. In those astonishing words, we shall 'be able to share the divine nature' (2 Pet. 1.3).

Such, then, is some hint of the profound and far-reaching truth which we acknowledge when we address God as Father. Though, as we have thought, each of us is united to this Father in a way we are instructed by our Lord to speak of and to *Our* Father. And here we are brought to an explicit affirmation of our solidarity with other men, all other men. The Fatherhood of God is the truth in which we find the authentic ground for our conviction about the brotherhood of man. It is true that many who refuse to accept any religious or transcendental view of reality are yet somehow convinced of the importance of human beings simply as human beings. It is the basis of what is today called Humanism. The Humanist quarrels with the believer because of the alleged or actual neglect of humanity which religious belief appears to involve. Yet whilst it must be admitted that a certain type of religiosity has all too often led to a neglect, if not a downright rejection of the specifically human values, it is equally true that genuine religious belief, above all in the Christian tradition, demands a total commitment to the promotion of human welfare. In an important sense, what Jesus was doing was to restore to the Jewish tradition that sense of the value of every single human being which had to some degree been obscured in the actual Jewish practice. It seems to be endemic in all forms of religion that the system, the code, the external expression or manifestation should tend to usurp the importance which ought to be given to the inner reality, the spiritual purpose which lies at the heart of true religion.

When Matthew's gospel places at the very head of the teaching of Jesus the first of the Beatitudes —'Happy are the poor in spirit'—he is, in effect, underlining a fundamental feature of the Christian message: the importance of the ordinary human being, the underprivileged, the outcast, the man who had no special place in society. The 'kingdom', the new version of God's ever-present concern for his children, unlike what the leaders of Jewry had come to make of the original Covenant, was above all promised to the shepherdless sheep before him. The first followers of Christ were content with an egalitarian society, distinguished for their mutual love, expressed not least in a sharing of resources. This idyllic state of affairs did not last for long. Paul's letter to the Corinthians, and still more the letter of James, make it clear that abuses had soon crept in. 'Do not try to combine faith in Jesus Christ, our glorified Lord, with the making of distinctions between classes of people' (Jas. 2.1).

In other words, if we recite the *Our* Father with

honesty, we must be expressing an inner conviction that the mere fact that we are children of a common father is the most important thing about us. Wealth, intellectual gifts, social distinction, professional success must be seen by comparison to be of little significance. As we have already thought, genuine prayer will lead us to realise more and more that what gives me my importance is the relationship that exists between me and God, a relationship of total dependence on a love that is total. But what is true of me is true of every single individual down the ages and across the world. This ultimately is the ground, whether or not it is the conscious motivation, of all humanitarianism. It also implies that the Christian should be outstanding in the service of his fellow-men. As we recite the Lord's Prayer it is well that we should emphasise to ourselves the truth that God is not only our Father but that he is *our* Father, that a recognition of his Fatherhood commits us to treating all men as indeed brothers. We remind ourselves of the sombre warning, or alternatively of the great encouragement addressed to those who treat their brethren—'the least of these little ones'—callously or sympathetically.

Since the Lord's Prayer is the most universal of all the formulas used in the Church's worship, it is appropriate here to add a few words about prayer in common. How well has an all-too-common attitude been summed up by Louis Evely:

We march into Church, notify God of what we want, and leave without bothering to listen to him, without consulting him or taking him into account, without giving him time to act, to answer, to change us ... (*Teach Us How to Pray*, p. 50)

Admittedly there are occasions when all we can do is to associate ourselves with what is being said in some stereotyped form of worship—psalms, reading, set prayers and hymns—without any great sense of personal involvement. Yet even here we can help ourselves by recalling that we are taking part in a great historic exercise, we are units in a vast crowd of witnesses who, for centuries, have thus praised and glorified God. If we reflect that even the more obscure psalms are part of the great Judaeo–Christian heritage in which man has sought to present to his Maker his offering of praise and thanksgiving, of adoration and petition, we can be helped and inspired to no small degree. But ought we not to ask ourselves whether we prepare ourselves sufficiently for our public worship? Most of us time our arrival at church to coincide as near as possible with the entry of the choir. It was Ronald Knox who said that we are quite happy to spend five minutes on a railway platform waiting for a train but are unwilling to spend that amount of time in church before the opening of the service. Yet those five minutes could make a very great difference to my attitude during the service. Despite the shuffling and the coughing going on all around me, I can be putting myself in the presence of God, recalling what I am about to embark on; recognising that, even amidst all the distractions which I know will come, I am nevertheless purposing to give this time to the unselfish exercise of offering to the majesty of God my tribute of humble service. There are those who go to church as to a theatre—to be entertained. If they do not find the service 'interesting' or 'inspiring' they almost want their money back. Yet, whilst it is to be hoped that we shall be helped by an inspiring preacher or a well-executed anthem, we must train ourselves to see that these things are but the icing on the cake. The true nourishment of my spiritual life is to be found in the sincerity and the generosity with which I offer myself 'a living sacrifice of praise'.

In other words, not the most professional choir nor the most eloquent minister can do our praying for us. We have all been present at great occasions in some splendid cathedral church, where we have felt uplifted by a rousing hymn-tune accompanied by the crashing chords of the organ. Are these necessarily more genuine acts of worship than, say, the singing of 'Rule Britannia' or 'Land of Hope and Glory' in the Albert Hall? There may well be more authentic religion practised by a handful of worshippers in a village church on a dark, cold morning. For in the end what matters is what each of us is contributing to the whole effort, the sincerity of faith, the generosity of a loving attitude to our fellows, the intellectual humility which recognises that, in face of the great mystery in which our God is shrouded, the only reasonable response we can make is a simple, uncritical sharing in a public act of self-dedication.

In this context of liturgical prayer, a word should be said about the changes that have taken place in the forms of service used by most of the major Christian churches. Whilst we must recognise that a familiar ritual comes to gather round it associations and overtones which render it precious, an excessive attachment, say to the 1662 Prayer Book or the Latin Mass, savours of what St John of the Cross calls 'spiritual luxury'. He criticises those whose prayer depends on the use of a particular crucifix or some similar object of piety. This can become a minor form of idolatry. The same is true of an exaggerated emphasis on this or that form of service—whether it be 'traditional' or 'experimental'. In either case, a species of Pharisaism, an insistence on the outward expression rather than on the inner meaning, may come in to impair the purity of my devotion. And when, as sometimes happens, the debate is conducted in terms of bitter and uncharitable invective, the only possible conclusion is that the supporters of whichever side have completely lost sight of the fact that any form of worship is simply the poor best that man can do to express the inexpressible. In this case, at least, despite Marshall McLuhan, 'the medium is not the message'.

Who art in heaven
The meaning of the word 'heaven' has become one of the debating-points of modern theology. It is suggested that the very use of the term implies an acceptance of the idea of a 'three-tier universe', with God 'up there', man here on this planet and the realm of the devils 'down there'. It may be doubted whether man has ever been quite so naïve as to take this sort of geographical language literally. The fact is that even the most sophisticated of us go on talking about the 'upper classes' and (though less openly) about the 'lower orders', about

a 'heavenly' day and the 'underworld' of crime, about the 'heights of ecstasy' and the 'depths' of despair, without attributing to them any localised signification. It is, after all, the 'lower orders' who tend to live in high-rise flats. . . .

It is that, because of the inevitably anthropomorphic language which we must use about God (since we have no other), we have a kind of feeling that the fact that God 'knows and sees everything' means that he has to have some sort of vantage-point from which he can do this. But the Jews were, in fact, less taken in by this sort of language than were, for example, the Greeks, who located their divinities on Mount Olympus. We have already quoted Psalm 139:

If I climb the heavens you are there
    there too if I lie in Sheol;
If I flew to the point of sunrise,
    or westward across the sea,
    your hand would still be guiding me ...

King Solomon was aware that 'the heavens and their own heavens cannot contain God' (1 Kgs. 8.26). If the psalmist says:

Yahweh has fixed his throne in the heavens,
his empire is over all (Ps. 103.19)

this did not mean that he was aloof, any more than the king, who sat on his throne, did not therefore move about among his people. 'Modern man' is often tempted to think that he is much cleverer than pre-Enlightenment or pre-Renaissance man. His vision of ultimate truth is equally limited. It is described in language that he happens to prefer.

'Heaven' is not a location. It is a quality of perfection. It is 'superior' to earth in the sense that it lacks the limitations to which we earthbound creatures are subjected. When, therefore, we are encouraged by our Lord to address our Father as being 'in heaven' or 'heavenly', we should recognise that this means that he possesses—is—all and more than all those perfections which traditional theology ascribes to him. Perhaps we may begin by suggesting that 'heavenly' can be rendered 'unearthly'. There is, as we know, a tradition in Christian mystical theology which insists that the truth about God can be stated only in negative terms. 'Unearthly' means that he is immaterial, first of all, and therefore free of all the limitations that being immersed in matter involves; uncreated; unrestricted 'by' space or time, so that terms drawn from our experience of this space–time world (as all our language is) are inapplicable to him: he is therefore present everywhere—or, rather, every point in space, like every second in time, is equally present to him. (He is, therefore, neither 'up' there nor 'down' here; the terms simply do not apply.) This restless, often chaotic, incomplete state of affairs which conditions so much of our human experience is altogether absent from the divine way of being. All that we recognise to be unworthy of human beings—the brutality, selfishness, stupidity, weakness, shortsightedness, ugliness of character and even of body, intolerance, hatred and a host of other defects—we see to be incompatible with the divine excellence. We must beware lest we appear to justify the cynical remark: 'God created man in his own image and man has returned the compliment.' It is so easy to 'project' upon God those ignoble qualities in ourselves of which we may not be aware but which we should recognise in others as being undesirable.

Although he has been mocked for his words, Robert Browning spoke wisely when he said: 'God's in his heaven, all's right with the world.' Obviously he would have been foolish indeed had he shut his eyes to the manifest iniquities and follies of his fellow-men. But in the sense that God remains ultimately in control of human affairs, bringing good out of their evil practices, 'writing straight with crooked lines', in the words of the Spanish proverb, Browning's, optimism reflects a thoroughly Christian attitude. When, then, we address God as our heavenly Father, we are—or should be—making an act of faith in his providential care. But it is an act of *faith*. All too often we cannot see the grounds for such trust. Yet, as the letter to the Hebrews reminds us:

> Only faith can guarantee the blessings that we hope for, or prove the existence of the realities that at present remain unseen. (Heb. 11.1)

When our Lord said:

> Your heavenly Father knows you need all these things. Set your hearts on his kingdom first and on his righteousness, and all these things will be added to you as well (Matt. 6.33)

he was not, so to say, bribing his followers. Their act of trust had to be an absolute thing, as we thought in an earlier chapter on the subject of petitionary prayer. It is not to be based on calculations of an earthly character. If we say, in effect, 'We have put the kingdom first; now give us what you promised', we are making it clear that we have been insincere in saying that we put the kingdom 'first'. All we have done is to make our putting it first conditional on being given something in return. Putting the kingdom first means a total surrender in absolute trust.

Hallowed be thy name

For the ancients, above all for the Jews, a name was much more than a sort of label distinguishing individuals one from another. It was descriptive of a person's character or function, so that, for example, to change a name was to indicate a change of destiny: Abram becomes Abraham, 'father of multitudes', Simon becomes Peter, 'Rock'. In the case of God, the Name had a profoundly religious significance. It is the Name which is loved—'they exult in you, those who love your name' (Ps. 6.11), 'hallowed'—'he shall hold my name holy' (Isa. 29.23). In Leviticus, we are told of a woman who blasphemed the name and cursed it' (24.11). When, therefore, we are encouraged to say 'hallowed be thy Name', what we are praying for is that the holiness of God be recognised by men and proclaimed. The Hebrew root from which the corresponding word is derived means, it would seem, 'separation'. In that sense God is the wholly Other, inaccessible, unapproachable. He is this because of his absolute purity which would be contaminated by the human contact. Hence the need to 'fear' God, to manifest that reverential awe which is a basic element in all religion. In this sense the fear of God is the beginning of wisdom. For this reason, 'hallowing the Name' is the first injunction of the Lord's Prayer.

Yet, since we are addressing our Father, it is, or should be, clear that our reverential awe is far from being the terror that petrifies or stuns the believer. Taken in the right spirit, it can and should be an inspiration and a summons to action. Faced with a majestic landscape, a sublime work of art, a supremely beautiful human being, a man may well be conscious of a sense of wonder and a feeling of his own littleness or unworthiness. But the sight should also be a challenge to him. If he is an artist he will seek to convey the vision into a painting, a musical composition, a piece of sculpture. In an immeasurably more profound way, the recognition of the utter perfection of God will not be crushing; it will be a spur to action. For all its insistence on the Otherness of God, his unapproachableness, the Bible also demands that we see the holiness of God as something for us to imitate. 'Be holy because I am holy.' Indeed, 'you have been sanctified and have become holy because I am holy' (Lev. 11.45,44).

The unapproachableness of God is in one sense a metaphorical expression. Even though it expresses the infinite 'distance' between him and his creatures, it in no way precludes that intimate nearness which links creature and Creator. 'I am the Holy One in your midst,' he says, as reported by the prophet Hosea (11.9). Here, of course, we are faced with the problem of the transcendence of a God who is yet totally immanent, transcendent to his creation because utterly independent of it, yet immanent because it is totally dependent on him. If we may so express it, our Lord is here refuting in advance the secularist tendency of much modern theology. We do no service to the secular order if we see it as the only reality, just as the humanist and the behaviourist in effect degrade human nature by denying to it any value other than that of its purely external activities. The best safeguard of human values is the recognition that they are a reflection of a higher system of values, not therefore to be despised (as some Christians have thought) but to be treasured all the more because of what they reflect.

When, therefore, we pray 'Hallowed be thy name', we are recognising the fact that creation itself partakes of the sacredness of its Creator. Of recent years we have come to a growing consciousness of the 'pollution' all about us, the poisoning of our atmosphere and our rivers, the scarring of our countryside, the desecration of natural beauty. The very term 'desecration' should be a reminder that we have failed to appreciate the sacred quality of God's earth. Of course he has made it ours, he has entrusted it to us—a truth which is expressed in characteristic language by the Bible.

From the soil God fashioned all the wild beasts and all the birds of heaven. These he brought to the man to see what he would call them; each one was to bear the name the man would give it. The man gave names to the cattle, all the birds of heaven and all the wild beasts. (Gen. 2.20)

Here, again, we see the significance of the 'name'. In giving names to the animals, man was expressing his control of them. But the control is not absolute. It must involve a recognition of the holiness of the Name of God, a holiness which is reflected even in the dumb animals. The legend of the forbidden fruit symbolises the profound truth that all nature must be enjoyed with a sense of respect, based on the recognition of God's ultimate overlordship. It is a legitimate extension of the idea behind the words 'hallowed be thy name' that we should see the holiness of God, not as something remote, having nothing to do with 'real life'. On the contrary, it is only by recognising the all-pervading majesty of God that we truly hallow his name.

Thy kingdom come

The reign of God, implicit in the mere fact of his creative power, is an eternal reality. Like his holiness, nothing we can do can in any way diminish or tarnish it. Our prayer is that that royal power should be effectively recognised and accepted by men 'on earth as it is in heaven'. But the reign of God is not a tyranny. It is true that the language of the Bible, especially in the Old Testament, sometimes seems to suggest that it is a cruel and oppressive domination. It is worth spending a little time on this problem since it has helped to colour many people's attitude to God. We need, then, to remember that much of the Old Testament was written for the Jewish nation at a time when they were fighting for survival in the midst of a group of powerful neighbours, practising various forms of idolatry, often accompanied by grossly immoral conduct under the guise of religious worship. Even if the earlier books of the Bible as we now have them were put together at a later period in the history of the Jewish people, they reflect a primitive stage in the spiritual development of the people.

To deter them from an acceptance of the ideas of other religions, the language of deterrence, of threatened terrors, was necessary. Yet, as we know, the language of love was intermingled with the language of hostility:

> I shall hide my face from them [he says],
> and see what becomes of them.
> For they are a deceitful brood ...
> I will hurl disasters upon them ... (Deut. 32.20-3)

are the words of Moses at the end of his days, knowing that after his death the Jews were 'sure to act perversely'. They need hardly be taken as explicit revelation of the divine nature.

A similar problem arises in connection with the savage commands which are attributed to God. Samuel, for example, is alleged to have said:

> Yahweh sent you on a mission and said to you, 'Go put these sinners, the Amelekites, under the ban and make war on them until they are exterminated'. (1 Sam. 15.18)

Again, we are told that God 'hardened Pharaoh's heart' (Exod. 4.21; 7.3), whilst the people complain:

> Why, Yahweh, leave us to stray from your ways and harden our hearts against fearing you? (Isa. 63.17)

These are examples of the way in which the Jews of old attributed to God actions or decisions for which men alone were responsible. Such an attitude was partly due to the fact that they were so convinced of the omnipotence of God that they felt that nothing that happened could happen not merely without his permission but, somehow, without his contrivance. It was also due, doubtless, to a not-uncommon human refusal to accept ultimate responsibility for our failures.

The point is more than a purely academic one. It involves the whole understanding of the nature of prayer. So often we feel that, having prayed for something to happen, we have done all that we can do. We have told God what we would like to happen. The rest is up to him. But of course the simple truth is that we are to a very large extent responsible for seeing that our prayers are 'answered'. When, for example, we say these words, 'thy kingdom come', we surely do not mean to suggest that God should somehow assert his authority by force; that he should terrify us into submission. God's rule is not that sort of thing. We have already thought that we are not puppets on a string, that God has made us responsible for the well-being of his creation, that he respects our dignity as free agents. God's kingdom will come only when and to the extent that men freely choose to obey his commands. But, again, those commands are not a set of arbitrary whims. They are simply the formulations of his loving designs for *our* well-being. In spite of the sort of pious language which suggests that our good behaviour 'pleases' God, that our sins 'offend' him, the blunt truth is that it is we who benefit from human virtue; we who suffer because of human vice.

Let us suppose that God's reign was established on earth. What, in effect, would this mean? It would mean that men's conduct was universally ruled by the great moral principles of altruistic care for others instead of by the prevalent selfish pursuit of individual or tribal advantage. It would mean the acceptance of the rule of law instead of the jungle-code of ruthless exploitation. It would mean peace instead of war, love instead of hate, compassion instead of cruelty. It would mean, in biblical terms, the establishment of the messianic age. And who would be the beneficiaries if not we human beings? Equally, who alone can bring this about if not we human beings? In other words, a sincere recital of this particular phrase of the Lord's prayer implies a personal commitment to playing my part in bringing about the state of affairs that I am praying for. It is no exaggeration to say that there is really very little point in reciting the words unless our recitation is accompanied by some determination to play our part in securing the coming of the kingdom. In practice this means a renewal of my resolve to accept the great moral principles as the groundwork of my own conduct. To the extent to which that is done, my prayer is already effective.

Thy will be done
If it were possible to sum up the achievement of Jesus in one sentence it would be in the words he addressed to his disciples at the well in Samaria:

> My food
> is to do the will of the one who sent me,
> and to complete his work. (John 4.34)

We have here not only a summary of the life and work of Jesus but a compendious expression of the Christian ideal. At the same time it is not unfair to say that there has been much misunderstanding about the precise meaning of the term 'God's Will'. Not a few identify God's will with whatever happens in the world—good or bad. But this is scarcely distinguishable from the Stoic teaching. In the Stoic view, the perfection of man consisted in living 'according to nature', accepting whatever happened without resisting. Man was compared to a dog tied to a cart. If the dog struggled against the motion of the cart, it only made things worse for itself, without achieving anything. Therefore the only sensible thing was not to struggle against Fate but to accept, uncomplainingly, 'stoically', fatalistically, whatever befell.

The authentic Christian view is much more subtle. There are two statements about God's will in the New Testament which can be taken in an absolute sense. St Paul says to Timothy: 'He wants everyone to be saved and reach full knowledge of the truth' (1 Tim. 2.4). And, writing to the Thessalonians, he says: 'What God wants is for you all to be holy' (1 Thess. 4.3). There are many things which happen in the world which are said to be God's will, evils of every kind from natural disasters to the many 'ills that flesh is heir to'. Yet it is certain that God cannot want any sort of evil to befall his creatures. God cannot will anything except what is good. Let us remember that, when we pray 'thy will be done', we go on to say 'on earth as it is in heaven'. In other words what we are praying for is that God's will, his will for man's salvation, for man's holiness (including man's happiness), shall be realised.

What then are we to make of all the tragic happenings in the world, including let us remember the sufferings and death of Christ, which are so often ascribed to God's will? We are told, in the letter to the Hebrews, that 'he learnt to obey through suffering' (Heb. 5.8). In the garden he accepted the 'will' of his Father that he should drink the cup of suffering. To understand what this sort of language means we need to distinguish carefully between what we have called the 'absolute' will of God— what God desires simply because it is good—and what we may call the 'permissive' will of God. In a previous section, we thought how the Jews ascribed to God everything that happened, so conscious were they of his omnipotence. Christian theology, whilst still believing in the divine omnipotence, interprets the situation very differently. We have already seen how God has, so to say, delegated to man the responsibility for developing the resources of the world. That delegation is a genuine reality. Therefore, whatever happens in the world happens because of man's choices, which God respects. At the same time, man has been given the necessary knowledge and the ability to make the right choices. When he does so, he is carrying out God's will, in the sense that he is doing what God would have him do. On the all-too-frequent occasions when, from stupidity or selfishness, through greed or passion or insensitivity, he chooses amiss, he is doing his own will directly. He is also thwarting what we have called God's absolute will. Since God has given man the power to act in accordance with that will, God is not to be held responsible for man's failure to live up to the ideals which he could achieve, if only he so willed. Equally, since God has chosen not to overrule man's decisions, since man's freedom is a reality, the choices which he makes are tolerated or permitted by a Father who, like a wise human parent, recognises that a valid psychological development will come about only by the exercise of a genuine responsibility. The son who is given an allowance by his father, with instructions and warnings about its purpose, cannot reasonably hold his father responsible if he ignores the warnings and spends the money recklessly. What the father wants is that his son shall use the money sensibly. Having given him the money he may be said to permit the misuse of it.

This is a human analogy of the situation as between ourselves and our heavenly Father. When, therefore, we pray that his will may be done 'on earth as it is in heaven', we are really praying for his absolute purposes to be realised. But, again, it is we who have the responsibility for carrying out that will, for making the right choices, for acting in accordance with the deepest and most authentic needs of our nature. For—and this is a point that calls for the greatest emphasis—God's will is not something that goes contrary to my own truest will. It may be that, in my shortsightedness or blind passion, I may feel a sense of resentment that 'my way' is not God's way. But, if I honestly believe in God's love for me, I cannot really doubt that even his sternest commands, as I may think them, are not directed to my own fulfilment. The sensible discipline which a wise parent requires of his child may, at the time, be resented by the child. But the resentment is nothing more than a sign of the child's immaturity and inexperience. So is it as between ourselves and

God. As the years pass we come to see that the only way to true happiness is through an acceptance of that moral law which is an important expression of divine love. Indeed, we recognise easily enough that if only other people were generous and thoughtful and reasonable and well-behaved, the world would be a much happier place. In effect, we should like everybody else to do God's will, even if we cannot be bothered to do it ourselves.

There is another important aspect of this whole question a study of which will shed further light on our problem. When our Lord said that his 'food' was to do the will of the Father who had 'sent' him, what are we to understand him to mean? We have already thought of the incarnation as God's pouring himself out in that final act of self-giving which is the culmination of the whole creative work of divine love. The effect of this self-emptying, to use the Pauline terminology, is the coming into being of Jesus of Nazareth, son of Mary and Son of the Father. Mary's son could be fully human only to the extent to which he was involved in the human experience. The 'will' of the Father who sent him was, in principle, that he should be so involved. What this meant in practice and in detail was that he should submit himself to the successive demands which that involvement might make on him.

Even before he was born, according to the account in St Luke's gospel, he was subjected to the bureaucratic machinery of the Roman Empire. After his birth, he came under the Law, which demanded circumcision, presentation in the Temple and, as we have thought, all the routine of the Jewish ritual. He was not less subjected to the demands, threats, requirements of the rulers of the day. He became a carpenter, not through any special choice of his own but because that was the trade of Joseph, the village carpenter of Nazareth. He was, henceforth, at the beck and call of his customers. He began his public mission, not because he himself had decided that the time was come, but because the Baptist appeared, preaching the gospel of repentance—a message which, as we have seen, he took as directed at himself as a member of the nation to whom the call was addressed. It was during his baptism, according to the common witness of all four evangelists, that he had an experience which he saw as a call to bear witness to the truth as he had come to understand it during the years of his obscurity. Following the call, he became involved in the complexities of the religious and political situation of the age, and was eventually crushed between the upper millstone of religious obtuseness and the nether millstone of political expediency.

In all this he was 'doing the will of God'. Now clearly we do not believe that God desired the obtuseness of the religious establishment or the timid compromise of Pilate or the brutality of the executioners. Only, if the sending of the Son was to result in a total involvement in that sort of situation, it was the Father's will that the Son should suffer the consequences, whatever they might be. Clearly, if men had done 'on earth' the will of the Father as it is done 'in heaven'; if men had accepted the teaching of Jesus, seen him as a reformer indeed but not as a subverter of the religious system of the day; if Pilate, having affirmed his innocence, had refused to be bullied by a threat to his own career, the will of the Father would have turned out, in detail, to have been different. Yet Christ's obedience would have been no less complete. He was prepared to accept whatever man might demand of him. Only so could he manifest to his fellow-men the completeness of his identification with them.

We are told that at the end of his forty days' fast in the wilderness he refused to satisfy his hunger by turning stones into bread. We are told that in the garden he prayed that it might not be necessary for him to go through to the end with this bitter task. We are told that he had only to ask the Father and angelic legions would come to his rescue. But if he had succumbed to that temptation; if the Father had 'let him off' and sent the angelic army, that would have been to destroy the whole significance of the Incarnation. Men are not in a position to work miracles to satisfy their physical needs; men are not rescued from tight spots by miraculous deliverers. Since he was a man, nor was he.

There is still another side to the activity of Jesus which will help us to understand a little more what doing the Father's will also involves. In the Acts of the Apostles, Peter is reported as having said that 'because God was with him, Jesus went about doing good and curing all who had fallen into the power of the devil' (Acts 10.38). The gospels are full of stories of the way in which he relieved distress of every kind. Doing the will of God does not mean passively accepting whatever may happen to one. It means actively joining in the struggle against evil, and not just moral evil. As we have already seen, the Christian is committed, even more than the

Humanist, to binding up the wounds of suffering humanity. When we pray 'thy will be done', we should, once again, be conscious of the challenge we are accepting. We should also spare a thought for all those who, without the inspiration of our Christian faith, are already doing the will of God. In the words of Teilhard de Chardin:

> Around us the 'natural' progress which nourishes the sanctity of each new age is all too often left to children of the world, that is to say to agnostics or the irreligious. Unconsciously or involuntarily, such men collaborate in the kingdom of God and in the fulfilment of the elect: their efforts, going beyond or correcting their incomplete or bad intentions, are gathered in by him 'whose energy subjects all things to itself'.

So, as the same author says:

> Try, with God's help, to perceive the connection —even physical and natural—which binds your labour with the building of the kingdom of heaven; try to realise that heaven itself smiles upon you, and through your works draws you into itself; then, as you leave church for the noisy streets, you will remain with only one feeling, that of continuing to immerse yourself in God. (*Le Milieu Divin,* pp. 66–7)

Such, then, is what the modern philosopher calls the 'cash value' of praying 'thy will be done'.

On earth as it is in heaven
This phrase refers not merely to the immediately preceding prayer, but to all three—the hallowing of

the name, the coming of the kingdom, the doing of the will. But it does also call for some further elucidation. At the same time, we have to face the fact that we are here up against a profound mystery; the whole problem of the relationship between 'this world' and the next, between time and eternity, between the perfected achievement of Christ and the ongoing struggle of Christians. What, for example, does Paul mean when he says:

> It makes me happy to suffer for you, as I am suffering now, and in my own body to do what I can to make up all that has still to be done by Christ for the sake of his body, the Church (Col. 1.24)?

In what sense can it be said that Christ's work is incomplete? Can we really do anything to add to that achievement?

We begin by recalling what that achievement is. In the traditional words it is the redemption of the world, the restoration to its ideal integrity of that world as it is seen in the eternal mind of God, an integrity from which (again using traditional language) it has 'fallen'. Certainly the world as we know it, not least our human nature, is far from being in that condition which could justify the words of the Bible: 'God saw all he had made, and indeed it was very good' (Gen. 1.30). As we look at the world today—two thousand years after the Incarnation, after the redemptive work of Christ—can we see any great improvement? Even in countries whose population is, at least nominally, Christian, do we see any lessening of violence, of corruption, of greed and selfishness, of the exploitation of the weak by the strong, of jealousy and treachery and every sort of meanness? Is the Humanist not justified in pointing to the crimes that have stained the history of the Church herself?

The answer is undubitable. This is why, beginning with Paul, members of the Church are called upon to 'make up all that has still to be done'. The truth is that the redemptive achievement of Christ, although in one sense it is final and complete, since nothing we can do will or could add to its value, is nevertheless an ongoing process. Christ laid down his life for all men. Only through his work will any individual be redeemed. Yet the redemptive process must clearly continue to the end of time, since it is only in the lifetime of any individual that, in his case, the redemption will take effect. The effectiveness of the redemption depends, then, on the response of the individual; a response that will be conditioned by many factors. One of those factors is the dedicated work of the Church, that is to say of the members of the Church at any given moment in history. 'Christ's work for his body, the Church' will always have to be done afresh, as generation after generation comes into the world and passes out of it. It is a sobering thought that the Church can impede just as it can further Christ's work. In that sense we can all, by our earnest and dedicated action, helped by the Spirit of God, do ever more for the spreading of the kingdom, helping on the final victory of Christ.

It is idle to pretend that we can have a clear and distinct idea of what this sort of language finally means. For we are here already engaged in those areas of speculation which go far beyond the reach of our conceptualising and even more beyond the scope of our language. Yet it is only those who hold that nothing is true unless it can be brought within the compass of human definition who will dismiss such talk as valueless. There is great perceptiveness in two sentences of Sir Thomas Browne's:

I love to lose myself in a mystery; to pursue my reason to an *O altitudo*!... Who can speak of eternity without a solecism, or think thereof without an ecstasy?

Yet we know that our activities on this earth do bear some relationship to the final perfection we call 'heaven'; that, even whilst our whole conscious experience is time-conditioned, it does nevertheless have some connection with that eternity which is unmoving now, in which the shifting scene against which we live out our lives on earth finds its abiding stability. It is in the wordless, imageless practice of prayer that we come to some apprehension of these truths.

Readers of scripture commentaries or works of theology may, if they are not familiar with the terminology, be puzzled by the word 'eschatological' which has become increasingly common even in books which are aimed at the average educated believer. 'Eschatology' is concerned with the situation at the 'end of the world', when there will be a 'new heaven and a new earth'. In many of the prophetic books of the Old Testament, we are presented with a vision of a marvellous age, when

Violence will no longer be heard of in your country,
nor devastation and ruin within your frontiers ...

No more will the sun give you daylight,
nor moonlight shine upon you,
but Yahweh will be your everlasting light,
Your God will be your splendour. (Isa. 60.18–19)

More emphatically, the author of the Book of Revelation declares:

The One sitting on the throne spoke: 'Now I am making the whole of creation new ... I am the Alpha and the Omega, the Beginning and the End ...'

In the new Jerusalem, the writer saw that:

there was no temple in the city since the Lord God Almighty and the Lamb were themselves the temple, and the city did not need the sun or the moon for light, since it was lit by the glorious radiance of God and the Lamb was the lighted torch for it. (Rev. 21.5,6,22,23)

These are attempts to describe the eschatological situation, attempts doomed to failure since the language is, inevitably, the language we use in our present situation. But the passages are quoted to indicate that the ultimate situation, the culmination of all human effort, helped by the grace of God, will be a total transformation into a completely different way of being—different and yet developing out of this earthly history. It is not like the chrysalis becoming the butterfly or the oak-tree growing out of the acorn. It is not even like the achievement of Browning's musician who, out of three sounds, fashions 'not a fourth sound but a star'. It is just a totally different way of being. In the meantime, we are to do all we can to prepare ourselves and this earth for what is to be.

Give us this day our daily bread
Having, as it were, set the scene by presenting us with a picture of the heavenly kingdom over which God rules, our Lord now encourages us to see our own needs in this larger context. We have already spent some time on the subject of petitionary prayer so that it is not necessary to say more about that aspect of these later items of the 'Our Father'. But there are two details of this particular request that may be usefully dwelt on. In the first place, 'bread' is to be understood as representing everything that man needs to support life. It symbolises and sums up the whole of man's material requirements. From the primeval curse:

> with sweat on your brow
> shall you eat your bread (Gen. 3.19)

to our Lord's retort to the tempter:

> man does not live on bread alone (Matt. 4.4)

the biblical usage is clear. It was therefore wholly fitting that, along with wine, bread should become the basic element in the institution of the Eucharist, the symbolic expression of the transmutation of our human nature into that supernatural, 'divinised', life which Christ came to give us in abundance. But, although the emphasis in the whole Christian tradition is on the superiority of that life, the fact remains that the natural, created realities are no less a gift from God than the gifts of grace and of glory. The whole Manichaean, puritanical approach

101

which would regard bodily satisfaction as somehow unworthy of human beings stems from a pre-Christian attitude, summed up in the Platonic formula *soma-sema*, 'the tomb' of the body, in which the soul is imprisoned and can be 'released' only by an increasing refinement and 'spiritualisation'. The story of the feeding of the five thousand, matched by the incident by the lakeside in Galilee when the Risen Lord is represented as preparing breakfast for his friends, should be sufficient to remind us that a faith founded on the Incarnation must honour the flesh, with all its needs, since this was the chosen vehicle for the final revelation of God.

This petition is no 'concession to human weakness'. It is integral to the whole Christian message. It is an explicit recognition of the truth that, whilst man does not live by bread alone, he cannot live without it. Therefore he rightly prays to be given this necessary sustenance. At the same time, we must ask the further question about the nature of this 'giving'. Does our Lord imply that bread will drop from heaven like manna in response to our prayer? Of course not. Apart from the fact that he himself had to work for his living as a carpenter, the whole of his preaching was delivered within the context of normal human activity. The parable of the sower; the picture of the housewife baking bread; the references to vineyards, fishing, business transactions and the like locate the gospel solidly in everyday life, the life where man has to produce his own food and drink.

What the words do serve to remind us of is that the whole of human activity does depend ultimately on the divine generosity. The success of man's efforts in whatever field—husbandry, scientific discovery, technological development, medical practice and all the other skills on which man's well-being depends—is possible only because of the natural resources, including the very brains that we apply to our problems, which are all given. The whole evolutionary process itself, whilst it has indeed developed the teeming wealth of our planet, has been able to do this because of certain intrinsic capacities that have been there potentially from the beginning of time. The chemicals that enable the acorn to grow into an oak-tree, the sun that ripens the corn, the oil that has been maturing in the depths of the earth these millions of years, the very force of gravity which conditions almost all our physical activities, all are 'given'. The simple words of our prayer—'give us our daily bread'—were answered 'in the beginning' when

God said, 'See I give you all the seed-bearing plants that are upon the whole earth, and the trees with seed-bearing fruit; this shall be your food'. (Gen. 1.29)

What, then, is the point of our asking? It is a reminder that God's gifts come to us, not directly, in a miraculous manner, but are administered through the hands of other human beings. Our daily bread comes to us from the shop, from the baker, from the farmer, from the corn-merchant. Whilst, then, we are making an act of faith in the generosity of God, we are also called upon to recognise that that generosity may be impeded or frustrated by human selfishness or greed. When the starving inhabitants of Ethiopia or Bangladesh pray

for their daily bread, they are, in effect, challenging
us to co-operate with God in seeing that their prayer
is answered. We, in the wealthy West, are blest. But,
even so, what is it that we have not been given St
John warns us:

> If a man who was rich enough in this world's
>   goods
> saw that one of his brothers was in need,
> but closed his heart to him,
> how could the love of God be living in him?
>   (1 John 3.17)

As always, then, we can make our prayer with sincerity and render it effective only if we are determined that we, in our turn, will emulate the
generosity of God. We do not pray, 'give *me my*
daily bread.' We are praying not for ourselves but
for the community. A purely selfish prayer is far
less likely to be 'answered' than a totally unselfish
one. Indeed, I can help to ensure that it will be
answered. How meaningful is my prayer if, after saying the words, I prevent it from being answered by
refusing to help those who are in greater need than
myself?

*Forgive us our trespasses as we forgive those who
trespass against us*
The best commentary on this petition has already
been made by Christ himself in the parable of the
unforgiving servant (Matt. 18.23–35). There is also
an interesting parallel in the book of Ecclesiasticus,
which summarises the argument implicit in this
prayer:

Forgive your neighbour the hurt he does you,
and when you pray your sins will be forgiven.
If a man nurses anger against another,
can he then demand compassion from the Lord?
Showing no pity for a man like himself,
can he then plead for his own sins?
Mere creature of flesh, he cherishes resentment;
who will forgive him his sins? (Ecclus. 28.2–5)

Once again we are reminded that our relationship with God, our whole spiritual life, is a reflection of our relations with our fellow-men. Those who think of religion as a form of escapism, as a flight from reality to some mythical region beyond this world, will find no justification for this attitude in the New Testament.

The most sublime manifestation of what is meant by forgiveness is to be found in our Lord's own words, as recorded by St. Luke, at the moment when he was being nailed to the cross.

Father, forgive them; they do not know what they are doing. (Luke 23.33)

There was no question here of his asking forgiveness for any sin of his own. At a time when the injustice and cruelty of men was culminating in this agonising suffering, he could find it in his heart not merely to forgive them himself, but to pray for their forgiveness by his Father. It is well that we should dwell on this prayer of his, linked as it is with the whole meaning of the Incarnation. The author of the letter to the Hebrews speaks of Jesus as 'Living for ever to intercede for all who come to God through him' (Heb. 7.25), an idea echoed by St

Paul when he says that 'he stands and pleads for us at God's right hand' (Rom. 8.34). In a mysterious sentence in the same letter, Paul says that:

> God dealt with sin by sending his own Son in a body as physical as any sinful body, and in that body God condemned sin. (Rom. 8.3)

In another passage Paul makes the extraordinary remark:

> For our sake, God made the sinless one into sin, so that in him we might become the goodness of God. (2 Cor. 5.21)

Although it is beyond the scope of this book to develop a full account of the doctrine of the Atonement, some brief summary of it is necessary if we are to appreciate the notion of forgiveness in a more than superficial sense. In short, then, we have to think of mankind as in debt to God, because it has failed to perform those 'duties' by which alone it can reflect that divine goodness and love which are the very basis of its own perfection and happiness. We talk of 'duties' to God, as though we were discharging some debt we owe him. But, as always, we need to bear in mind that nothing we say or do can either benefit or harm God. Analogously, when we say that a young man has 'betrayed' or 'disgraced' his ancestors by his conduct we are speaking metaphorically. Nothing he can do now can make any difference to what they were or achieved. But he has harmed himself by failing to live up to their standards. In the same sort of way, by failing to live up to God's standards, we have inflicted on ourselves the wound of sin. Human nature has become sinful, to the extent that we are not only constantly committing sin, but because there is in all human beings that weakness, that proneness to sin, which Augustine called *fomes peccati*, the tinder which can so easily catch fire. By becoming man, by taking a 'body as physical as any sinful body', Jesus used the very instrument of sin to overthrow its power.

Are we not still in the area of metaphor? Can we clarify our ideas a little more? This we can do by reminding ourselves what sin essentially is. It is not something I do, or say, or think, or refuse to do—though these may be its outward manifestations. In essence sin is the attitude of will of a human being who says No to God. What Jesus did was, as we have already seen, in every human situation to say Yes to the Father. He could have waved a sort of magic wand and healed our human nature from outside. But, in accordance with his general way of dealing with men, he wished man's cure to be effected from within. Instead of a rebellious humanity, God saw in Jesus a man who was totally obedient to his will. We have already seen what this meant in practice. It is sufficient here to suggest that, in his prayer for his executioners, Jesus was interceding for all mankind. 'Father, forgive them, they do not know what they are doing.' Up to a point, of course, we do. But there are so often so many extenuating circumstances. If the Roman soldiers had really known who it was they were treating in this way, would they have gone on doing what they were doing? If we realised the consequences of our present conduct, if we were sufficiently clear-sighted to estimate the inevitable effects of our getting drunk before getting into the driving-seat of a car, would we still do it?

In brief, and returning to the Lord's Prayer, if we plead extenuating circumstances in our case, if we expect to be forgiven, are we prepared to look for similar extenuating circumstances in the conduct of those who have offended us, hurt us, damaged us in some way. 'Forgive in the measure in which we forgive.' We can hardly dare to embark on that particular prayer whilst nourishing a grievance. And, above all, the example of Christ on Calvary may help.

Lead us not into temptation
At first sight, the implication of this prayer would seem surprising, if not altogether shocking. Are we to suppose that the Father is the sort of being who might lead us into temptation if we did not pray to him? Surely not.

Here, as we have thought in an earlier section, we have an example of the way in which the Jewish mind ascribed directly to God's action events of various kinds which are really the outcome of human choices. What we are asking is that we may not be led into temptation from whatever source; that God will not allow us to be tempted. We can make our prayer with great earnestness, knowing our own weakness. It can be an expression of genuine humility. At the same time, if we are honest in our request, we are also undertaking not to lead ourselves into temptation. As we have seen throughout our study of this prayer given to us by Jesus, we are not encouraged to shuffle off on to God the responsibilities which we are called upon to cope with, and for which we are assured by St Paul we shall be given the necessary strength. In his own experience he had been plagued by some problem which remains an enigma to us. It was, as he tells us, something humiliating—'a thorn in the flesh'. When he begged to be relieved of the trouble, he was told: 'My grace is enough for you: my power is at its best in weakness' (2 Cor. 12.7–9). The meaning of this is, presumably, that when we are most conscious of our need for the divine help, it is then most likely to be forthcoming. At any rate, generalising from his own experiences, Paul assured the Corinthians: 'You can trust God not to let you be tried beyond your strength and with any trial he will give you a way out of it and the strength to bear it' (1 Cor. 10.13).

The problem is complicated by the fact that we regard temptation as a prelude to sin; almost as possessing some of the wickedness of the sin itself. Yet that this is not necessarily the case is clear from the story of the 'temptations' of Jesus. In so far as we are able to understand what the events were that lay behind the story as we now have it, this much can be said. It is clear that in each of the three incidents described Jesus, in his human consciousness, was given the opportunity to give the answer to the various suggestions that were made to him. We have already seen how, if he had, *per impossibile*, yielded to the natural desire to satisfy his hunger by making use of powers beyond the normal range of man's ability and turning stones into bread, he would cease to be subjected to the ordinary conditions of human life. The Incarnation would, so to say, have been suspended for his benefit. He would have been going against his Father's will. More; he was to preach the importance of complete confidence in the Father. How could he have preached such a lesson in all honesty if he had himself failed to practise what he was preaching. 'You must not put the Lord your God to the test' (Matt. 4.7) meant, of course, that our trust in God, as we have already thought, must be an absolute thing, not dependent on whether he gives me here and now what I would like.

Another aspect of this topic concerns the true meaning of 'temptation'. As we have just said, for most of us it appears as a prelude to sin. Even if we resist the temptation, we feel that the struggle itself is an indication of some weakness in us. If only we were less imperfect, we should have no problem in handling our temptations. But if we reflect that, in being tempted, we are in fact being tested, we may be able to console ourselves with the thought that the tougher the struggle, the greater the strength displayed, even whilst we recognise that we can achieve what we do achieve only with the grace of God. If I am put through a stiff examination, the object of the exercise is not to find out how ignorant I am but rather how much I know. When a test-pilot takes up a new aeroplane, he is out to prove how much it can do, not how badly it is made. In other words, we may take our Lord's words in this particular petition as a kind of shorthand, meaning: 'Let me not be put to the sort of temptation that I shall not be able to resist. In so far as I am tested, I believe that your power will be available to me.'

Finally, we may relate what we have just been

thinking to our earlier discussion about the 'permissive will' of God, since it provides a good illustration of what that term means. Our temptations (or trials or tests) have their origin either in some interior weakness of my own—the consequence of earlier failures or some psychological maladjustment—or else are due to external factors—the malice of others, the lack of some essential material goods, the threat from natural forces of one sort or another—causing sickness or some other indisposition. Now none of these evils can be ascribed to the absolute will of a benevolent Father. They are due, directly or indirectly, to that dislocation in the world, the general recalcitrance of men and things which characterises a 'fallen' condition. Yet, as we also know, faced with courage and generosity of spirit by us, they can develop a quality of mind and heart which a less demanding state of affairs does not produce. The sufferings of others give us the opportunity to exercise those qualities of sympathy and devotion which are important elements in a fully rounded personality. Such are some of the reasons why we can accept the idea that God is not a harsh tyrant by permitting such things to happen. This is not, of course, the whole answer. But as far as it goes it can be of help.

But deliver us from evil

Little needs to be said by way of commentary on this final appeal. It is a natural cry from the heart of Everyman, looking at the evils in the world about him. It seems hardly necessary to discuss whether the Greek means evil in general or 'the evil one'; evil, so to say, hypostatised in Satan. However we envisage evil, we all desire to be rid of it, even whilst we recognise that it will not disappear from the face of the earth merely because we make this prayer. What we can pray for with complete conviction and sincerity is to be delivered from that personal enslavement to the evil of sin which St Paul refers to in his letter to the Romans:

> You know that if you agree to serve and obey a master, you become his slaves. You cannot be the slaves of sin that leads to death and at the same time slaves of obedience that leads to righteousness. You were once slaves of sin, but thank God you submitted without reservation to the creed you were taught. You may have been freed from the slavery of sin but only to become 'slaves' of righteousness. (Rom. 6.16–18)

THANKSGIVING

No study of the prayers of Jesus would be complete without some mention of his attitude of thanksgiving. We are especially familiar with this in connection with the institution of the Eucharist, and with the anticipation of it in the various stories of the feeding of the five thousand. Jesus 'took the bread and gave thanks'. Do we always remember that the very word *eucharist* is an abiding expression of our own thanks—our gratitude to the Father for the gifts of bread and wine which, by his power, have become an even greater Gift, the ever-present, ever-renewed action whereby the power of God-in-Christ becomes available to us all. The best way of ensuring that that power becomes effective in us is by recognising it for what it is, the self-giving of

Jesus. Initially, he gave himself in the Incarnation; he gave himself throughout his life, by his never-ending service of his fellow-men; he gave his life for us on the Cross. Because he gave himself so completely, he was given back everything and more than everything. He was given back the fulness of life in the Resurrection. And now, because his self-giving is no longer limited to the conditions of his mortal life, he can give himself totally to all who approach him. Aware of what this Gift means, we accept it with hearts filled with gratitude. 'If only you knew what God is offering,' he said to the woman at the well (John 4.10). If only we knew....

In two passages, Teilhard de Chardin draws together what the nature of our Thanksgiving should be:

You have come down, Lord, into this day which is now beginning. But, alas, how infinitely different in degree is your presence for one and another in the events which are now preparing and which all of us together will now experience! In the very same circumstances which are soon to surround me and my fellow-men you may be present in small measure, in great measure, more and more or not at all.... The gift you ask of me for these brothers of mine—the only gift my heart can give them—is not the overflowing tenderness of those special, preferential loves which you implant in our lives as the most powerful created agent of our inward growth; it is something less tender but just as real and of even greater strength. Your will is that, with the help of your Eucharist, between me and my brother-men there should be revealed that basic attraction (already dimly felt in every love once it becomes strong) which mystically transforms the myriads of rational creatures into (as it were) a single monad in you, Christ Jesus. (*Hymn to the Universe*, pp. 28, 92)

The cynic has defined gratitude as a lively anticipation of favours to come. The lover knows that he can express his gratitude only by a return of love and service. The believer, conscious that his whole life has been and continues to be an endless stream of gifts, recognises that one of the greatest gifts of all is that he has been enriched so that, in his turn, he can assist the course of divine self-giving.

One of the most striking expressions of gratitude in the whole of the gospels can be found in the words Jesus spoke immediately before working the miracle of raising the dead Lazarus to life:

Father, I thank you for hearing my prayer.
I know indeed that you always hear me,
but I speak
For the sake of all those who stand round me.
    (John 11.42)

As we offer up to God our petitions for our various needs, can we find it in our hearts to say 'I know you always hear me'? Do we not rather wait to see whether we have got what we want before being able to say thank you? If the example of Jesus means anything to us, it means that an attitude of thanksgiving should accompany even our most desperate cry for help. The very fact of my praying at all to God is meaningful only if I really have faith in his power to give and in his loving desire for my total happiness. This is the meaning implicit in the words of Jesus:

> Everything you ask and pray for, believe that you have it already, and it will be yours. (Mark 11.24)

This is one of those sayings of our Lord which poses a tremendous challenge to our Christian faith. The reaction of the material-minded—and which of us is not to a greater or less extent subject to that meanness of heart?—is to say, in effect: 'There, I prayed for my friend's health, and he seems to be rather worse; I prayed for the success of some perfectly good enterprise, a parish activity for a good cause, and it turned out to be a complete failure. It would be dishonest to say that I got what I prayed for.' In the superficial sense, of course, that is true. But Christianity is not a superficial affair. It takes us right down to the depths of reality. If, at the superficial level, my experience contradicts the words of Jesus, do I therefore conclude that he was deluded or, to save his face, that he has been misquoted? Or am I prepared to admit that the failure is in me, in the sense that I am still far short of that absolute confidence in God and his love which assures me that every single hair of my head is not only known to God but is more precious to him than it is to myself. In the end, Christianity adds a dimension to life far more significant than any Einsteinian fourth dimension. It is the dimension of eternity in which God's love is not frustrated by man's malice, that heavenly kingdom to which my prayers contribute even though, on earth, nothing *seems* to come of them.

> God is spirit,
> and those who worship
> must worship in spirit and truth. (John 4.24)

If the test of my worship is the achievement of some immediate and obvious benefit, I am losing sight of that profound utterance of Christ's:

> Have I not told you that if you believe you will see the glory of God. (John 11.40)

We have to train ourselves to see the glory of God across and through the tragedies of this world. The supreme testimony to this truth is the Cross of Christ through which came not only his own resurrection but the salvation of mankind.

There is a short passage in St John's gospel which might almost be a commentary on the foregoing remarks.

> Now my soul is troubled:
> What shall I say:
> Father, save me from this hour?
> But it was for this very reason that I have come to this hour. (John 12.27)

We are again at the heart of the mystery of human experience of Christ. Although he believed totally in the love of the Father, he was none the less capable of the normal human reaction to the threat of suffering and death. His soul was 'troubled' here, as, in the garden, he was to be 'in anguish', 'sorrowful to the point of death'; 'sadness came over him and a great distress'. The strength of his faith and trust were no anodyne. He could feel the terror which is the common experience of most men at some stage in their lives. To suggest, therefore, that there is almost something glib about his utterances concerning the answer to prayer is to lose sight of these features of his life which the gospel recounts to indicate his fellow-feeling with us. An attitude of continuing grateful trust is possible only when it is tested. If it is merely a response to getting what I want, as and when I want it, this is no more than an exercise in self-interest.

THE PRIESTLY PRAYER OF CHRIST

Before we begin to comment on this sublime prayer which constitutes the seventeenth chapter of the fourth gospel, it will be useful to pause for a moment to reflect on the nature of that gospel. It has been widely regarded as the least 'historical' because the most 'theological' of the four. There is an obvious sense in which this is true, though there are a number of details scattered about which indicate that the author was by no means unconcerned about facts. In the sense that it is much more of a meditation on the significance of the events of Christ's life, his words and works, this is a description which hardly needs to be insisted on. Because it is such, the most natural attribution of its authorship is to the 'beloved disciple', John the apostle, writing or, more probably, dictating towards the end of his long life. This traditional attribution is, we suggest, more natural than any other because it implies the activity of someone who, having been closer in heart and mind than any of the other followers and friends of Jesus, could be expected to see more deeply into his teaching and to appreciate the significance of all that he did. He has, of course, organised his material in a highly individual way, precisely in order to bring out most effectively the splendour of what he had seen. Indeed, the best commentary on his gospel has been provided in the first of the three letters ascribed to him.

> Something which has existed since the beginning,
> that we have heard
> and we have seen with our own eyes
> that we have watched and touched with our
>   hands;
> the Word, who is life—
> this is our subject.

Whether, then, we have in the chapter the very words of Jesus or those words as reflected in and through the mind of John does not matter. If we are to have an interpreter, we could not do better than listen to one who was so close to his Master.

Let us, then, briefly recall the setting in which John has put this great prayer. Before the supper, at which Jesus had instituted the holy Eucharist, he had washed the feet of his friends, as a symbol of the service of love which his followers were to pay to one another. He had encouraged them with words of love and of reassurance, to face the hostile world which would persecute them. He had promised the Spirit to lead them to the complete truth. The final, astonishing words of inspiration were

> In the world you will have trouble,
> but be brave:
> I am the world's conqueror. (John 16.33)

He then turns to pray to the Father, beginning with the words:

Father, the hour has come
glorify your Son
so that your Son may glorify you.

Earlier in that same week, he is reported as having
said

Now the hour has come
for the Son of Man to be glorified.
I tell you most solemnly,
unless a wheat grain falls on the ground and dies,
it remains only a single grain;
but if it dies it yields a rich harvest. (John
  12.23–4)

Here, of course, we are presented with one of the
central paradoxes of the Christian message: the
message of triumph through failure; of death
through life; of glory through shame. The other
three evangelists describe in some detail the struggle
which Jesus underwent in the garden, the prayer
that he might not have to drink the cup of suffering
and death. Not so John. Even as the troops gathered
round Jesus to arrest him, we are told that they fell
back at the words: 'I am he.' Even then, John implies, the power of God was manifest in Christ, so
that he went freely to imprisonment and execution.

What is this 'glory' of which John speaks so
often? It would seem to be inevitable to think of it
as associated both in the mind of Jesus and of his
interpreter John, reared in the Jewish tradition,
with the abiding presence of God in the Shekinah,
the visible glory of God in the cloud, appearing in

the desert (Exod. 16.10), on Sinai (Exod. 24.16), filling the tabernacle (Exod. 40.34), finally filling Solomon's temple (1 Kings 8.10). But that glory is now revealed in Christ (John 1.14; Heb. 1.3), transiently on earth, in the Transfiguration, but permanently 'in heaven'. John, looking back across the years to the events of the life of Jesus but, above all, to the Resurrection, can see how, in the words of the risen Lord, reported by another evangelist, 'it was ordained that Christ should suffer and so enter into his glory' (Luke 24.27). In the striking metaphor of the wheat grain Jesus, as reported by John, suggests the splendour of the field of golden grain that has come from the 'death' of the seed, and its burial in the dark ground where it germinates unseen.

The glorification of the Son, then, is the final outcome of a process of stress and apparent failure. It is no sudden irruption of God into his world, it is no triumphant entry of Christ into an earthly kingdom. It is the reverse of a coin of which the obverse alone is visible to us in our temporal existence. It was only 'after Jesus had been glorified' (John 12.16) that John and the rest could understand the significance of the events of the life of Jesus. So we, living in the darkness of faith, cannot see the glory of the Son. Yet that same faith assures that the very frustrations and contradictions of life contain the elements of the glory that is to be revealed even in us (Rom. 8.18). It is the glory of Christ, revealed in his members because of the complete union existing between him and those who have come to know him and to share his work. We share in that work by living a life dedicated to the glory of God.

As the prayer continues, Jesus says:

I have glorified you on earth
and finished the work
that you gave me to do. (John 17.4)

How, in effect, does the life of Jesus 'glorify' God?
How can we, in our turn, do the same? The lesson
of the human achievement of Jesus is that 'giving
glory to God' does not imply any very extraordinary
or spectacular activity. It is true that he did, from
time to time during the later stages of his life, heal
the sick, give sight to the blind, raise the dead. But
taking his life as a whole, we see it as a very ordinary
affair of carrying out a routine job in an unexciting
way. Throughout his life, he responded to the demands of the human situation in a totally human
way. Even his miracles must be seen as primarily
due to a human desire to alleviate suffering where-
ever he encountered it. If, at the close, his death
seems to us sensational and dramatic, we need to
reflect that, in that brutal age, it was little more
than a routine execution. The fact that, in the history of the world, it has proved to be the supreme
drama, is in itself a kind of hint of the glory that
was concealed in it. If the Cross has indeed become
'glorious' it is because it was the final manifestation
of Christ's self-identification with humanity in the
extremity of its suffering. He was identified with all
who suffer a violent death, who suffer injustice,
indeed with all sons of Adam who suffer and die. No
one is excluded from the saving work of Jesus, no
one therefore from the possibility of sharing in his
glory. Here a passage from St Paul provides the best
commentary:

We know that by turning everything to their good God co-operates with all those who love him, with all those that he has called, according to his purpose. They are the ones he chose specially long ago and intended to become true images of his Son, so that his Son might be the eldest of many brothers. He called those intended for this: those he called he justified, and with those he justified he shared his glory. (Rom. 8.28–30)

For the glory of Christ is no self-centred self-seeking, self-satisfied state. The glory of Christ must be identified with his love, as the Father's glory is indistinguishable from his love. That is why in this final prayer, in the last hours of his life, when he is looking forward to his return to the Father, the thoughts of Jesus are concerned with those he is to leave behind.

I pray for them:
I am not praying for the world
but for those you have given me,
because they belong to you;
all I have is yours
and all you have is mine,
and in them am I glorified. (John 17.9–10)

The sentence 'I am not praying for the world' is not to be understood as though the world was excluded from the compassion of Christ. It is true that, throughout John's gospel and his letters there is a certain ambivalence in his use of the term. The world is sometimes that creation which Christ came to save. 'God loved the world so much that he gave his only Son'. Indeed:

God sent his Son into the world
not to condemn the world,
but so that through him the world might be
    saved. (John 3.16–17)

But it is also understood as meaning those who re-
ject or refuse to acknowledge Christ.

Though the light has come into the world.
men have shown they prefer
darkness to light. (John 3.19)

In a well-known passage, John describes more explicitly what he understands by 'the world':

The love of the Father cannot be
in any man who loves the world,
because nothing the world has to offer—
the sensual body,
the lustful eye,
pride in possessions—
could ever come from the Father,
but only from the world.
And the world with all it cares for
is coming to an end. (1 John 15–17)

Yet not even the world in this sense is beyond redemption. When, therefore, Jesus says 'I am not
praying for the world', it is as though, in human
fashion, his attention was so taken up with the needs
of this small group of his friends that he could not
look beyond them and their future. He has already
warned them of the 'trouble' that is to come. In his
prayer he is seeking to reassure them that, whatever
befall, the grace and power of God will always be
at their disposal. His prayer is not, then, so much a

petition to the Father, as a way of letting them know of his concern. Indeed

> while still in the world I say these things
> to share my joy with them to the full. (John 17.13)

UNITY

Jesus now introduces a theme which has become increasingly familiar in recent years:

> Holy Father
> keep those you have given me true to your name
> so that they may be one like us ...
> I pray not only for these
> but for those also
> who through their words will believe in me.
> May they all be one.
> Father, may they be one in us
> as you are in me and I am in you ...
> With me in them and you in me
> may they be so completely one
> that the world will realise that it was you who
> sent me. (John 17.11,20–1,23)

Familiar as the words are, it is well that we should dwell on them here since they remind us of the necessary basis of unity—truth and love. It is an unfortunate fact of history that the grave divisions within the Body of Christ have come about, not because different Churches or groups of Christians have deliberately rejected something which they believed to be true, but because they have failed to perceive the nature of the truth which in their intolerance they have sought to 'defend' by persecuting and anathematising those who preferred to state

the truth as they saw it in a different way. It is a
cliché familiar to all students of the literature of
Church history that 'heresy' springs from intellectual pride. In so far as this is true, it is only a part
of the truth. The deeper reason would seem to be
that the divisions have come about much more because of a failure of love. In the never-to-be for-
gotten words of the letter to the Ephesians,

If we live by the truth and in love
we shall grow in all ways into Christ, who is the
    head
by whom the whole body is fitted and joined to-
    gether
every joint adding its own strength, for each
    separate part to work
according to its function.
So the body grows until it has built itself
up, in love. (Eph. 4.15–16)

The truth we have accepted—the truth which we
must, of course, defend and cherish—is the revelation of God in Christ. In the nature of things, as we
have already seen, that truth is wholly beyond the
capacity of the human mind to embrace. The best
we can do is to remember that our poor attempts at
definition can at best only hint at the infinity of
meaningfulness that is not, cannot be, encapsulated
in any formula, however carefully worded, however
officially guaranteed. How often, in the course of
the history of the Church, has it not turned out that
some 'heretical' opinion has contained in it some
aspect of the total truth which had been omitted or
neglected in the 'official' version. If only both sides

in some passionate controversy had remembered the injunction to live by love as well as by truth, points of view would not have become embattled positions from which one side or the other was unwilling to retreat, until forced to do so by the march of history.

The condemnation of Galileo is a classical case. Another is the general repudiation of the theory of evolution because it was thought to contradict the Bible. A third, and perhaps saddest of all, is the argument that went on for centuries about the nature of the Eucharist. It has been the saddest of all precisely because it concerned the sacramental expression of Christ's love. If men had borne two things in mind: first, that we are here dealing with a sublime truth which is clearly beyond our comprehension and, secondly, that we could remain true to whatever its 'meaning' might be only to the extent to which it brought us closer in spirit and did not separate us from our fellow-Christians, it seems impossible to believe that the venomous hatred of the controversies surrounding this precious gift could ever have been engendered. True, so long as man's mind remains limited and his capacity for love sadly restricted; so long is this picture of quarrelsome Christendom likely to endure. But we all do well to meditate on the reason why Christ prayed for the unity of his followers: 'so that the world may believe that it was you who sent me'. Let us remember too that we are called upon to manifest the unity of the very Godhead, the fulness of mutual comprehension, the totality of outgoing love, which is the life of the three divine persons, whose absorption one in another is so absolute that, remaining themselves, they yet constitute a unity which is not merely unbreakable; even intellectually it cannot be divided up.

Such is the pattern according to which we are to seek to establish the unity of the visible Body of Christ. We are to envisage a situation in which, because of historical circumstances, cultural or psychological differences, and a hundred other causes, separate traditions have developed in our interpretation and expression of the truth revealed by Christ. Yet, overarching all these differences and welding them into a genuine communion of minds and hearts, is the abiding consciousness that, in our several ways, we are all honestly seeking to bear witness to Christ. Nor is this to advocate a vague syncretism. On the contrary, if we are honestly prepared to listen to one another in a spirit of charitable truth-seeking, based on a genuine effort to understand what the other person or party is trying to say, we are more likely to arrive at a mutual clarification of ideas than if we go on simply asserting a number of statements as the only valid way of stating the truth.

Nor should we limit the scope of the prayer of Our Lord to ecclesiastical unity. Just as the unity of the Godhead is to be the prototype of the Church's unity, so this in turn should serve as an example to mankind at large. Certainly, one of the most effective ways of achieving the unity of Christians is to set them to work together to healing the wounds of stricken humanity. Just as the Jews failed in their universal mission by thinking of themselves as the Chosen Race, separated by God himself from the gentile world which they misunderstood and despised, so have Christians in their turn betrayed Christ by being so absorbed in their own internal divisions that they have left little or no time to concern themselves with the more universal problem of the 'salvation' of the world, the bringing to fulfilment and perfection of the whole of mankind and, in fact, the whole of God's creation. In thinking of our Lord's own spiritual formation we thought of such passages as the words of Isaiah:

I will make you the light of the nations so that my salvation may reach to the ends of the earth. (Isa. 49.6)

What Jesus thought of ecclesiastical exclusiveness is clearly shown in the parable of the Samaritan, a member of the hated heretical and alien people, who came to the help of an unfortunate victim after the official representatives of Judaism had ignored his plight. Although he had declared that his own personal mission was confined to the land of Israel, he did commission his followers to carry his message to all the nations. All Christians profess their faith in a 'Catholic' Church. Too often they forget that a true catholicism is incompatible with a parochial or sectarian mentality.

MISSION AND DEDICATION

As you sent me into the world,
I have sent them into the world,
and for their sake I consecrate myself
so that they too may be consecrated in truth.

We have seen more than once in the course of this study what the 'sending' of Jesus by the Father meant, in theory and in practice. His mission was to carry out the will of the Father, not least by teaching the truth about him. We recall the words he spoke to Pilate;

> I was born for this, I came into the world for this: to bear witness to the truth. (John 18.37)

It was because he insisted on bearing witness to the truth that he came to his death. He becomes, as it were, a sacrificial victim, dedicated to the truth, the truth which so many men rejected. Now he prays that that same witness may be continued by his followers; that they may have the same dedication to the truth. Just as, in the other accounts we have of the Last Supper, we see Christ, in effect, ordaining ministers of the Sacrament—'do this as a memorial of me' (Luke 22.19)—so here he ordains them as ministers of the Word.

In other words, the mission of the Church, the mission to preach the gospel, to administer the sacraments—the life-giving Word, the life-giving Body—are a continuation, a prolongation, of the original mission; the sending of the Son by the Father. The words of the letter to the Hebrews form a fitting commentary:

> You who wanted no sacrifice or oblation
> prepared a body for me
> You took no pleasure in holocausts or sacrifices
> for sin; then I said:
> just as I was commanded in the scroll of the
> book:
> 'God, here, I am! I am coming to obey your will.'

The author goes on to apply this quotation from Psalm 40 to Jesus:

This *will* was to be made holy for us by the *offering* of his *body* made once and for all by Jesus Christ ... By virtue of that one single offering, he has achieved the eternal perfection of all whom he is sanctifying. (Heb. 10.5–7; 10.14)

CONCLUSION

Jesus has made clear to his followers his self-dedication to the truth, a dedication he calls on them to copy. He has made it clear that their vocation is a sharing in his own mission; the truth they are to preach is his truth, a truth which is much more than a factual statement. It is indeed a revelation of the truth about his Father, but that truth goes far beyond anything that can be expressed in human language. In the words of the letter to the Hebrews:

The word of God is something alive and active; it cuts like any double-edged sword; ... It can judge the secret emotions and thoughts ... everything is uncovered and open to the eyes of the one to whom we must give an account of ourselves. (Heb. 4.12–13)

To attempt to reduce the 'truth' of Christianity to a set of propositions is to diminish, not to enrich, its true value. The public language of the Creed is obviously necessary in any form of organised religion. But the ultimate test of unity is not the willingness to subscribe to a formula. It is the spirit of faith in the reality which the words vainly attempt to define that is the truly cohesive force. In any family, as in any community, there have to be certain accepted rules or conventions. But the family is united not by observing the conventions but by the spirit of love which transcends any outward expression or manifestation of it. When Jesus said:

> By this love you have for one another everyone will know that you are my disciples (John 13.35)

he was stating a truth which has all too often been lost to sight. 'Dedication to the truth', then, means dedication to a life based on the recognition of the power of love which, in the unforgettable words of Dante: 'moves the sun and the other stars'. That love, as we have thought, is expressed in the creative activity which calls into being and supports the universe. It is expressed supremely in the self-emptying which enables God to come down to our level, to involve himself in our affairs, to share our experiences. By the side of this towering truth, theological definitions are paltry indeed.

So, as he comes to the end of his prayer, Jesus refers to the primordial fact:

> Father
> I want those you have given me
> to be with me where I am,
> so that they may always see the glory
> you have given me
> because you loved me
> before the foundation of the world. (John 17.24)

We recall the opening words of this same gospel:

In the beginning was the Word:
the Word was with God
and the Word was God.

We recall the words of the letter to the Hebrews:

He is the radiant light of God's glory and the
perfect copy of his nature, sustaining the universe
by his powerful command. (Heb. 1.3)

It is in words such as these that we come to the very
heart of the Christian message. It is not until we
have come to base the whole of our lives on an
acceptance of this truth, however dimly we may
understand its meaning, that we have begun to be
authentically Christian. But once we have, then
faith and hope and charity come together in one
simple commitment. We believe in the Word, because the Word is God's own truth; because that
truth has been revealed to us in Jesus, we can place
our entire hope in him, not least because whatever
disasters may befall, whatever terrors may threaten,
we know that they have befallen him; and our love
goes out to him, because of what he is and what he
has done. It goes out, too, to all our fellow-men,
because we see in them other representations of that
humanity which has been ennobled by his Incarnation.

THE PRAYER IN THE GARDEN

After the sublimity of the utterances recorded in the
Priestly Prayer we have just been reflecting on,
the story of the events in Gethsemane come as a
reminder that, if Jesus could know the heights, he
could equally plumb the depths:

> My Father, if it is possible, let this cup pass me
> by. Nevertheless let it be as you, not I would
> have it. (Matt. 26.39)

For the traditional theologian, the words provide
a puzzle. How can the 'I' of the Incarnate Word
be somehow antithetical to the 'you' of the Father?
But theological investigations are not always the
best way to an appreciation of the sort of truth we
encounter in the experience of Jesus. If it is true,
as we have been insisting, that, in the words of
Bonhoeffer: 'In Jesus Christ the reality of God
entered into the reality of this world', then the
reality of God will somehow be encountered in the
realities of this world. And amongst those realities
not the least prevalent is that of human suffering
and its attendant human reactions of fear and
shrinking. How God's involvement in this situation
is to be reconciled with what is called the divine
'impassibility' is a problem for the theologian. For
the ordinary believer it is enough to recognise that
the human experience of Jesus included the
reactions to which we have referred. He felt the
sadness of the coming parting, the 'anguish' and
'sudden fear' of which Luke and Mark speak, the
loneliness which made him turn for comfort to his
friends—only to find them asleep. Inevitably, being
the sensitive human being he was, he longed desper-
ately that it might not be necessary for him to drink
the cup of suffering. As a son, how could he not
give expression to this desire in a prayer to the
Father? Yet, heartfelt as that prayer was, he would
have been untrue to himself and his whole teaching had he not uttered it within the context of his

total surrender to the Father's will. Because he was man, he could not but feel what he did feel. Feeling it, he could not but give utterance to what he felt. But, being the man he was, dedicated to the living-out of the human destiny he had assumed in the beginning, he could not but acknowledge the over-riding importance of the will.

Still, we cannot ourselves help asking the question: Was it not possible for the Father, even now, to alter the scenario, to make it easier—less painful —for Jesus? We already know in broad outline why, despite the 'omnipotence' of God, this was something he could not do. For, as we have already seen, God has chosen to limit his 'omnipotence' in the sense that the freedom of man, given by God, has been given absolutely. God does not overrule it. What man chooses to do, that he chooses to do. It is a fact that not even God can alter, any more than he can alter his own nature. If, then, Judas, Caiaphas, Pilate and the rest chose as they did, the consequences would be what they would be. Paradoxically, the last person on whose behalf God would intervene by working a miracle by 'sending twelve legions of angels', was Jesus. For, as we have already thought, Jesus had no privileges which lifted him above the common human lot.

We believe, of course, that God's involvement in the world in the life and work of Jesus Christ, has profoundly altered the situation. But true as that is, it is not true in the sense that the nature of temporal reality has been radically changed. What it does mean is that, in consequence of the redemptive work of Christ, man can use his involvement in human affairs to help on that final fulfilment which will come about at the end of time. Meanwhile, we have to do the best we can (in every sense of the word 'best'), just as Jesus himself had to. Bonhoeffer said, in a phrase which has been much misunderstood, that we must live in the world 'as though God did not exist'. What he meant was not that we should doubt the existence of God nor that we should cease to pray to him, but that we should not think of him as someone who would come to our rescue when we are in a tight corner, who would compensate for our shortcomings or stupidities. Not only is such an idea contrary to the evidence of history. It is not borne out by the life of Jesus. Kipling has summed up the situation in a poem entitled *The Sons of Martha*, which ends with these lines:

And the Sons of Mary smile and are blessed—
   they know the Angels are on their side.
They know in them is the Grace confessed, and
   for them are the Mercies multiplied.
They sit at the Feet—they hear the Word—they
   see how truly the Promise runs;
They have cast their burden upon the Lord, and
   —the Lord he lays it on Martha's Sons!

It is this sort of false religion which Bonhoeffer condemned when he pleaded for a 'religionless Christianity'. For, as he said, 'it is not the religious act that makes the Christian, but participation in the sufferings of God in the secular life'. The most traditional of theologians have always talked of the sufferings and death of God, but they have been reluctant to draw the logical conclusion. God suffered and died in Jesus precisely because he had put himself at the mercy of the secular world. Once more it is Bonhoeffer who has emphasised an important aspect of the truth about God, Christ and his world when he says: 'God lets himself be pushed out of the world on to the cross.'

It would be idle to pretend that we are not here faced with one of the most perplexing aspects of the whole mysteriousness of God. Nor should we ever lose sight of the fact that, whilst God's involvement in his creation is one important way in which we can best appreciate his immanence, he remains transcendent in the sense that that creation can in no way affect his nature. And, of course, that nature is itself totally beyond our comprehension. It is impossible for us to make any sense of the idea of a being that is unaffected by the flux of temporal events, a being who is unchanging yet not static, energising yet never impaired, endlessly giving yet never diminished, spiritual yet calling into existence this material universe. One element in the whole puzzle is due to the timelessness of God's knowledge. People have created difficulties for themselves by talking about God's *fore*knowledge. But God does not *fore*see. As we have already thought, God's eternity means that every detail of the cosmic process is equally present to the mind of God. He does not see them in the future or in the past. Therefore, when men wonder why, since God knows what is going to happen, he does not prevent the various disasters that afflict the world, this is a pseudo-problem. The history of the world does not unroll before God's eyes like some filmed epic. He does not see men and women working away at some endless tapestry. The finished article is just as present to him as the activity which produces it. In the context of the prayer of Jesus in the garden, therefore, we need to remember that the Father saw the glory of the Resurrection just as truly as he saw the suffering and death. He saw the achievement *in* the struggle, the victory *in* the defeat, the triumph *in* the disaster. And if the achievement, the victory, the triumph are, as we must believe, immeasurably more splendid than the struggle, defeat and disaster are squalid and painful, even though the latter are the price of the former, then it is not cruel to permit these latter. The lover is forever boasting of what he is prepared to do and suffer for his beloved. Is he to be deprived of the challenge?

In brief, then, when Jesus prayed 'if it is possible, let this cup pass me by', he was praying that the future might not be the future. But in God's eternity, what we call past, present and future are equally real. We cannot change the past or the present. And, although in one sense we can change the future, we cannot make what is to be not to be. Nor can God.

THE HOLY SPIRIT
On two occasions, at least, we are told that Jesus prayed for the Holy Spirit to come upon the apostles.

I shall ask the Father
and he will give you another Advocate
to be with you for ever
that Spirit of truth
whom the world can never receive

since it neither sees nor knows him. (John 14.16–
17)

He breathed on them and said:
Receive the Holy Spirit. (John 20.22)

The lengthy discourse after the Last Supper is, as
we know, studded with references to this same
Spirit, and since St Paul says

when we cannot choose words in order to pray
properly, the Spirit himself expresses our plea in
a way that could never be put into words (Rom.
8.26)

it seems fitting to add some reflections on the place
of the Holy Spirit in the life of the Christian.

We begin with some words which, at first sight,
seem a little puzzling:

It is for your own good that I am going
because unless I go,
the Advocate will not come to you;
but if I do go,
I will send him to you ...
When the Spirit of truth comes
he will lead you to the complete truth ...
and he will tell you of the things to come. (John
16.7,13)

In what sense could it be 'good' for the apostles
that their Master should leave them? Would it not
have been better, had it been possible, for him to
stay with them until the Church had been success-
fully launched? But to think like this is, once again,
to fail in an understanding of God's ways with men.

So long as Jesus was on earth, it was inevitable that his followers would fail to live up to their own responsibilities. The decisions would always be left to him. But we have to learn to grow up, to shoulder our own responsibilities, to make our own decisions.

Moreover, so long as Jesus was there, his message would be construed simply in terms of his background, his individual experience, his Jewishness. As we know, even after he had left them, they still found it difficult not to see the whole Christian thing within a Jewish context. It was a necessary feature of the Incarnation that it had to occur in a specific cultural and religious situation. But, since its effects were to be world-wide, the presentation of it had to assume a universal dimension. 'Jesus' had to leave them so that 'Christ' in all his fulness might be preached. The process by which the Galilean followers of Jesus became the world-wide missionaries, preaching the Good News to all the nations, would be controlled by the Spirit of truth, leading them to the complete truth. Not that even they, in their lifetime, would come to a full understanding of the message entrusted to them. The Church herself will never exhaust the riches of which she is the custodian. Always the Spirit will be leading her on to a deeper grasp, a developing formulation, of the unchanging teaching of Christ. Always, therefore, must she be sensitive to the Spirit. That is to say, her members must be for ever open to the Spirit, open in a totally open-minded, open-hearted readiness to listen.

Here, above all, the importance of prayer is manifest—the prayer of the individual, seeking to know the will of God for him, and the prayer of the community, of the Church as a whole, reading the signs of the times, preserving what is essential from the past but ever aware that God's revelation is an ongoing, unending activity. The truth that makes us free will liberate us from the sort of blinkered nostalgia which imagines that the only way to defend the truth is to go on insisting that the 'tradition of the elders' must be maintained in every detail and at any cost. It was this sort of mummified religion which Jesus himself set out to criticise. He came, indeed, not to destroy it but to fulfil it; to bring out its real spirit; to liberate it from the cramping restrictions of a soulless routine. 'Justice, mercy, good faith', as Jesus said, can so easily be lost sight of in a religious practice which consists in a repetition of liturgical formulas or doctrinal statements with no regard for the inner spirit by which alone these external rites become expressions of a loving worship.

PEACE

The last prayer of Jesus recorded in the gospels is: 'Peace be with you' (John 20.19). It was, of course, no more than the conventional greeting. *Shalom*, though on our Lord's lips it was far more than that. As he had said on an earlier occasion

> Peace I bequeath to you,
> my own peace I give you,
> a peace the world cannot give, that is my gift to
>   you. (John 14.27)

The meaning is clear. The peace that Jesus gives is not to be equated with what we normally think of as peace—an absence of strife, a readiness to work together, an orderly way of life—important as these are. Christians certainly must do all they can to promote such a situation. But that the peace of Christ is independent of external happenings is clear from the fact that he says to his friends

I have told you all this
so that you may find peace in me.
In the world you will have trouble ... (John 15.33)

St Paul describes the peace of God as 'so much greater than we can understand' (Phil. 4.7). It is the peace of the 'messianic age', so often promised in the Old Testament. It is more than what is called the peace of a good conscience. It is the peace that comes from an utter conviction of the power and love of the Father as revealed in Christ. It is a spiritual condition, independent both of external pressures and interior feelings. The Christian has no assurance that he will not have to suffer the manifold evils that beset mankind. If anything, he may have to put up with persecution, mockery, ostracism. Like his Master, he will feel all these things. But, just as the 'glory' is, as we have thought, revealed across the sufferings and humiliation of Christ, so will peace be possible for the Christian in a situation of violence, terror, disaster of every kind.

In the end, of course, the peace of God, since it is beyond our comprehension, is not a state of mind into which we can argue ourselves. It depends on a deepening faith in the reality of Christ's achievement. That achievement is something that is fully realised only in that situation in which the triumph of the Risen Lord is manifest throughout the whole of creation; a creation transformed by its complete incorporation into Christ. Yet a perseverance in prayer, with its concomitant growth in an abiding awareness of God's action in the world, can help to establish in our hearts the kind of trust in the loving Providence of the Father which will enable us to maintain in the depths of our being a sense of peace which is essentially undisturbed by the storms that wash over us, the anxieties and disappointments that beset us, the inevitable grief that will come our way. At the same time, we have to reckon with the fact that a 'peaceful disposition' is, to no small extent, due to a quality of temperament which is not universal. If I am so blessed, I can and should be grateful. But it does not necessarily mean that I have achieved the peace which Jesus promised to his followers.

Gerard Manley Hopkins, a poet with a different temperament, wrote of this problem in the words:

When will you ever, Peace, wild wooddove, shy
        wings shut,
Your round me roaming end, and under be my
        bough?
When, when, Peace, will you, Peace? I'll not play
        hypocrite
To own my heart: I yield you do come some-
        times; but
That piecemeal peace is poor peace ...

But the real answer comes in a later poem:

Across my foundering deck shone
A beacon, an eternal beam. Flesh fade, and
    mortal trash
Fall to the residuary work; world's wildfire, leave
    but ash;
      In a flash, at a trumpet's crash,
I am all at once what Christ is, since he was what
    I am, and
This Jack, joke, poor potsherd, patch, match-
    wood, immortal diamond
      Is immortal diamond.